Author biography

Ishwar Singh, Rahul Pawar, Birinder Pal Kaur and Kanchan Pawar have more than 12 years of teaching experiances. Ishwar Singh has worked as Assistant Professor under the the Department of Mechanical Engineering in Punjab Technical University. Rahul Pawar has worked as computer engineer in the multinational companies. Birinder Pal Kaur has worked as Lecturer under Central Institute of Plastic Engineering and Technology, Amritsar. Kanchan Pawar is presently working as a research scholar in the field of education. They all are working as a team to provide quality education to the students.

101 Interactive Classroom Teaching Activities

Engage, Inspire and Empower the students with the Interactive Classroom Teaching Activities for the Modern Age

Ishwar Singh & Rahul Pawar

ISBN 1234567890123345
© Ishwar Singh & Rahul Pawar 2023

Published in India 2023 by Pencil

Contributors:
Co-Author: Birinder Pal Kaur
Co-Author: Kanchan Pawar

A brand of
One Point Six Technologies Pvt. Ltd.
Unit no. 26, Ground Floor, Building A1,
Wadala Truck Terminal Road,
Near Post Office, Antop Hill, Mumbai - 400037
E connect@thepencilapp.com
W www.thepencilapp.com

CONTENTS

Foreword

Interactive classroom teaching activities have become an essential part of modern education. The traditional model of a teacher-centered classroom is gradually being replaced by a student-centered approach, which emphasizes the active involvement of students in the learning process. Interactive teaching activities are designed to facilitate this involvement by encouraging students to participate, collaborate, and engage in critical thinking.

The purpose of interactive teaching activities is to make learning a more engaging, fun, and effective experience for students. These activities can take many forms, including group discussions, debates, problem-solving exercises, and hands-on projects. They can be used to teach a wide range of subjects, from science and math to literature and history.

Preface

Interactive classroom teaching activities are educational techniques that encourage active participation and engagement from students during classroom instruction. These activities can take many forms, such as group discussions, peer-to-peer learning, hands-on experiments, simulations, and games. They are designed to facilitate a collaborative learning environment where students can share ideas, ask questions, and work together to solve problems.

Interactive classroom teaching activities are important because they provide students with opportunities to develop critical thinking skills, communication skills, and teamwork skills. They also help to keep students engaged and motivated, which can lead to better retention of information and improved academic performance.

There are many different types of interactive classroom teaching activities that teachers can use to enhance their lessons. The choice of activity will depend on the subject matter, the age and abilities of the students, and the teacher's teaching style. Some popular examples include debates, role-playing exercises, project-based learning, and interactive quizzes.

Acknowledgements

We are eternally grateful to our parents, Shri Pal Singh, Shri Amarjit Kaur, Shri Tilak Raj Pawar and Shri Saroj Pawar who took in an extra mouth to feed when they didn't have to. They taught us discipline, tough love, manners, respect, and so much more that has helped us to succeed in life. We truly have no idea where we'd be if they hadn't given us a roof over our head whom we desperately needed at that age.

101 Interactive Classroom Teaching Activities

1. Quiz Games

- Kahoot: This is a popular game-based learning tool that enables instructors to build and host quizzes in a fun and engaging manner. Students may use their smartphones or tablets to participate in the quiz, and the platform delivers real-time feedback on their responses.

- Quizlet Live: This game is ideal for studying vocabulary concepts or other subjects. Students are separated into teams and work together to answer questions as fast and precisely as possible.

- Jeopardy: This iconic game show format may be simply modified for the classroom. Teachers may set categories and questions depending on the topic they've covered in class, and students can compete in teams to see who can get the most points.

- Who Wants to Be a Millionaire: Another famous game show style that may be modified for the classroom. Students may work independently or in teams to answer questions and climb the ladder to become a "millionaire".

- Plickers: This is a fun and engaging approach to engage students in class quizzes. Each student is given a unique QR code card that they may hold up to indicate their response. The instructor may then scan the cards using a smartphone or tablet to rapidly analyse student replies.

2. Brain Teasers and Riddles

Brain teasers and riddles are fantastic interactive classroom exercises that may test students' critical thinking skills and enhance their problem-solving ability. Here are several examples:

- What has a heart that doesn't beat? (Answer: An artichoke)

- I am kidnapped from a mine and put up in a wooden case, from which I am never freed, and yet I am utilised by practically every individual. What am I? (Answer: A pencil lead)

- What begins with an E, finishes with an E, but only has one letter? (Answer: An envelope)

- The more you take, the more you leave behind. What am I? (Answer: Footsteps)

- I am not living, yet I grow; I don't have lungs, but I require oxygen; I don't have a mouth, but I need water to survive. What am I? (Answer: Fire)

- What belongs to you yet others utilise it more than you do? (Answer: Your name)

- What has a head and a tail, but no body? (Answer: A coin)

- What is constantly in front of you but can't be seen? (Answer: The future)

- What passes across cities and farms, yet never moves? (Answer: A road)

- What has a neck but no head, two arms but no hands? (Answer: A shirt)

3. Debates

Debates are a wonderful interactive classroom exercise that may help students strengthen their critical thinking, research, and public speaking abilities. Here are some recommendations on how to conduct a classroom debate:

- Choose a subject: Choose a topic that is related to the curriculum and that students will be interested in. It is ideal to choose a subject that has two obvious sides, so that students may investigate and debate for and against it.

- Assign teams: Divide the class into two teams, one to argue for the issue and one to argue against it. This will push students to investigate and prepare their arguments.

- Investigate: Encourage students to investigate the issue fully utilising a range of sources, such as books, journals, and internet resources. This will help them construct well-informed arguments.

- Develop arguments: Students should develop arguments for their team, concentrating on the major points that they wish to emphasise. They should also anticipate counter-arguments that the other side may offer.

- Set ground rules: Establish clear guidelines for the discussion, such as the length of time each side has to deliver their points and the sequence in which they will speak.

- Conduct the debate: Conduct the argument in a disciplined and orderly fashion. Each side should deliver their reasons, followed by a response from the opposite team. Encourage pupils to be courteous and to listen closely to the points offered by the opposite team.

- Assess: After the discussion, ask students to assess their performance and that of their teammates. This will help students recognise their strengths and flaws and develop their abilities for future arguments.

- Debates can be an interesting and engaging opportunity for students to learn about important subjects and enhance their critical thinking and public speaking abilities.

4. Group Discussions

Group discussions are a terrific interactive classroom exercise that may help students enhance their critical thinking, listening, and communication skills. Here are some pointers on how to conduct a group discussion:

- Choose a subject: Choose a topic that is related to the curriculum and that students will be interested in. It is preferable to choose a subject that is open-ended and promotes diverse opinions.

- Set ground rules: Establish clear ground rules for the debate, such as respecting each other's viewpoints, listening intently, and avoiding interruptions.

- Assign responsibilities: Assign roles to students, such as a facilitator who will direct the conversation, a timekeeper who will ensure that the discussion remains on course, and a note-taker who will record crucial points.

- Provide prompts: Provide students with suggestions or questions to steer the conversation. This will encourage students to think critically and share their opinions.

- Encourage participation: Encourage all pupils to join in the conversation, especially if they are timid or silent. You may achieve this by asking open-ended questions, allowing students to build on one other's ideas, and providing a supportive atmosphere.

- Foster discussion and disagreement: Encourage students to question one other's views constructively and to investigate diverse viewpoints. This will help students build their critical thinking abilities and learn how to communicate effectively.

- Describe and assess: At the conclusion of the conversation, describe the important themes that were covered and ask students to evaluate their performance. This will help students understand their strengths and shortcomings and develop their abilities for future group talks.

Group conversations may be a great approach for students to express their ideas, learn from one other, and enhance their communication and critical thinking abilities.

5. Role-Play

Role-play exercises are a fun and dynamic approach to engage kids and help them build their communication, problem-solving, and cooperation skills. Here are some recommendations on how to plan a role-play session in the classroom:

- Choose a scenario: Choose a scenario that is relevant to the curriculum and that students will be interested in. This might be a real-life circumstance, a historical event, or a speculative scenario.

- Assign roles: Assign roles to students, such as various characters in the scenario, and offer them with background information and goals.

- Provide parameters: Provide instructions for the role-play, such as how long it should run, what the goals are, and what the rules are for interacting with other characters.

- Encourage improvisation: Encourage pupils to improvise and adapt to unexpected events throughout the role-play. This will help students build their problem-solving and communication abilities.

- Facilitate the role-play: Facilitate the role-play by offering suggestions, asking open-ended questions, and steering the conversation to ensure that all students are involved.

- Debrief and assess: After the role-play, debrief with the students and ask them to evaluate their performance. This will help students assess their strengths and limitations and develop their abilities for future role-play sessions.

Some examples of role-play exercises may include a mock trial, a job interview, a historical reenactment, or a negotiation. Role-play exercises may be an excellent approach to engage kids and help them improve their communication and problem-solving abilities.

6. Mind mapping

Mind mapping is an interactive classroom practise that may help students enhance their critical thinking, creativity, and organising abilities. Here are some recommendations on how to plan a mind mapping activity:

- Choose a subject: Choose a topic that is related to the curriculum and that students will be interested in. It is preferable to choose a subject that is difficult and comprehensive.

- Provide supplies: Provide children with tools for mind mapping, such as paper, colored pens, and markers. You may also utilise internet tools for digital mind mapping.

- Explain the concept: Explain the idea of mind mapping to pupils and present them with examples. Encourage kids to be creative and think beyond the box.

- Set a time restriction: Set a time limit for the activity to keep kids engaged and motivated.

- Encourage collaboration: Encourage students to work in groups and cooperate on their mind maps. This will help students enhance their collaboration and communication abilities.

- Share and discuss: After the mind mapping task, encourage students to share their maps with the class and discuss their thinking process. This will help students improve their presenting and public speaking abilities.

- Evaluate: Evaluate the mind maps depending on the criteria you have created, such as originality, organization, and depth of analysis.

Mind mapping may be a useful technique for students to visually organize their ideas, enhance their critical thinking abilities, and express their creativity. It may also be a fun and interesting classroom exercise that stimulates teamwork and debate.

7. Presentations

Presentations are an engaging classroom practise that may help students enhance their communication, research, and presenting abilities. Here are some recommendations on how to plan a presenting activity:

- Choose a subject: Choose a topic that is related to the curriculum and that students will be interested in. It is preferable to choose a subject that is open-ended and promotes diverse opinions.

- Provide parameters: Provide rules for the presentation, such as the duration, structure, and criteria for assessment.

- Assign responsibilities: Assign duties to students, such as a presenter, a researcher, a graphic designer, and a timekeeper. This will promote teamwork and guarantee that all areas of the presentation are addressed.

- Investigate: Ask pupils to investigate the issue carefully and to utilise credible sources. You may present them with a list of resources or websites to assist them get started.

- Rehearse: Encourage students to rehearse their presentation numerous times to ensure that they are confident and prepared. You may give criticism and coaching to help them improve their presenting abilities.

- Provide visual aids: Encourage students to utilise visual aids, such as PowerPoint presentations, films, and photographs, to improve their presentation.

- Evaluate: Evaluate the presentations based on the criteria you have specified, such as organization, content, delivery, and visual aids.

Presentations may be a useful approach for students to communicate their ideas, research, and analysis with their classmates. It may also be a fun and interesting classroom exercise that stimulates teamwork and debate.

8. Collaborative Projects

Collaborative projects are an engaging classroom activity that may help students enhance their cooperation, problem-solving, and communication abilities. Here are some recommendations on how to plan a joint project activity:

- Choose a project: Choose a project that is related to the curriculum and that students will be interested in. It is preferable to choose a project that demands diverse abilities and viewpoints.

- Assign responsibilities: Assign roles to students, such as a project manager, a researcher, a graphic designer, and a presenter. This will promote teamwork and guarantee that all areas of the project are addressed.

- Set goals and objectives: Set specific goals and objectives for the project and convey them to the students. This will help them remain focused and motivated.

- Provide guidelines: Provide parameters for the project, such as the timetable, structure, and criteria for assessment. Encourage kids to work together and to communicate effectively.

- Encourage creativity: Encourage pupils to be creative and to think beyond the box. This will help students strengthen their problem-solving and critical thinking abilities.

- Monitor progress: Monitor the progress of the project and give comments and help as required. This will help pupils remain on course and conquer any hurdles they face.

- Evaluate: Evaluate the project depending on the criteria you have specified, such as originality, collaboration, and quality of the final result.

Collaborative projects may be an excellent approach for students to work together and enhance their cooperation and problem-solving abilities. It may also be a fun and interesting classroom exercise that stimulates creativity and innovation.

9. Scavenger Hunts

Scavenger hunts are an engaging classroom exercise that may help students enhance their critical thinking, problem-solving, and collaboration abilities. Here are some pointers on how to plan a scavenger hunt activity:

- Choose a subject: Choose a theme for the scavenger hunt, such as a historical era, a scientific issue, or a cultural event. Make sure the topic is related to the curriculum and age-appropriate.

- Create a list: Create a list of things or clues that pupils need to discover or solve. Make sure the list is hard yet feasible and offer clear directions.

- Set boundaries: Set limitations for the scavenger hunt and make sure children are aware of any sites that are off-limits. This will secure their safety and avoid any interruptions.

- Assign teams: Assign teams of pupils to work together on the scavenger hunt. Make sure each team has a variety of abilities and personalities to foster cooperation and teamwork.

- Provide resources: Provide items that children will need for the scavenger hunt, such as a map, a compass, or a digital camera. This will boost their problem-solving abilities and make the scavenger hunt more enjoyable.

- Monitor progress: Monitor the progress of the teams and give tips or direction if required. This will help pupils remain on course and conquer any hurdles they face.

- Evaluate: Evaluate the scavenger hunt based on the criteria you have specified, such as originality, collaboration, and completion time.

Scavenger hunts may be an excellent approach for children to learn in a fun and engaging manner. It may also be a wonderful approach to encourage cooperation, critical thinking, and problem-solving skills.

10. Crossword Puzzles

Crossword puzzles are an interactive classroom activity that can help students develop their vocabulary, spelling, and critical thinking skills. Here are some tips on how to organize a crossword puzzle activity:

- Choose a topic: Choose a topic that is relevant to the curriculum and that students will be interested in. It is best to select a topic that requires students to use critical thinking and problem-solving skills.

- Create the crossword: Create the crossword puzzle using a template or an online crossword maker. Include a mix of easy and difficult clues to challenge students.

- Provide clues: Provide clues for each word in the crossword puzzle. You can provide definitions, synonyms, or antonyms to help students solve the puzzle.

- Assign teams: Assign teams of students to work together on the crossword puzzle. Make sure each team has a mix of skills and personalities to encourage collaboration and teamwork.

- Set a time limit: Set a time limit for completing the crossword puzzle. This will help students stay focused and motivated.

- Monitor progress: Monitor the progress of the teams and provide hints or guidance if needed.

This will help students stay on track and overcome any obstacles they encounter.

- Evaluate: Evaluate the crossword puzzle based on the criteria you have established, such as completion time and accuracy.

Crossword puzzles can be an effective way for students to learn and practice their vocabulary and spelling skills. It can also be a fun and engaging classroom activity that encourages critical thinking and problem-solving skills.

11. Board Activities

Interactive board activities are a great way to engage students and create an interactive learning experience. Here are some examples of interactive board activities that you can use in the classroom:

- Jeopardy-style game: Create a Jeopardy-style game using an interactive board that includes questions from the curriculum. This is a fun way to review concepts and reinforce learning.

- Virtual field trip: Use an interactive board to take students on a virtual field trip. This can be a great way to explore different parts of the world, learn about historical events or visit museums and art galleries.

- Collaborative brainstorming: Use an interactive board to encourage collaborative brainstorming among students. This can be a great way to generate ideas, solve problems or develop a group project.

- Interactive story time: Use an interactive board to read and explore interactive stories. This can be a fun way to encourage reading and literacy skills while engaging students in a creative way.

- Mind mapping: Use an interactive board to create and explore mind maps. This is a great way to help students visualize and organize their thoughts and ideas.

- Collaborative drawing: Use an interactive board to encourage collaborative drawing activities among students. This can be a fun way to explore creativity and develop teamwork skills.

Interactive board activities can be a great way to engage students and create an interactive learning experience. It allows students to be more involved in their learning process, encourages collaboration and creativity, and helps them to retain information better.

12. Interactive Storytelling

Interactive storytelling is a fun and engaging way to encourage reading and language development among students. Here are some tips on how to organize an interactive storytelling activity in the classroom:

- Choose a story: Choose a story that is appropriate for the age and reading level of your students. You can choose a classic story, a folktale, or a contemporary story that is relevant to the curriculum.

- Create a script: Create a script that includes interactive elements such as sound effects, gestures, and audience participation. This will help to engage students and make the story come alive.

- Use props: Use props such as puppets, costumes, or visual aids to enhance the storytelling experience. This will help to keep students engaged and focused on the story.

- Encourage participation: Encourage participation from students by asking questions, inviting them to make sound effects, or allowing them to act out parts of the story. This will help to keep students engaged and involved in the storytelling process.

- Reflect: Take time after the story to reflect on what was learned and how it relates to the curriculum. This will help students to connect the story to their learning and retain information better.

Interactive storytelling is a fun and engaging way to encourage reading and language development among students. It allows students to be more involved in the storytelling process, encourages creativity, and helps to develop their language skills.

13. Interactive Whiteboard

Interactive whiteboard activities are a great way to engage students and create an interactive learning experience. Here are some examples of interactive whiteboard activities that you can use in the classroom:

- Collaborative drawing: Use an interactive whiteboard to encourage collaborative drawing activities among students. This can be a fun way to explore creativity and develop teamwork skills.

- Jeopardy-style game: Create a Jeopardy-style game using an interactive whiteboard that includes questions from the curriculum. This is a fun way to review concepts and reinforce learning.

- Virtual field trip: Use an interactive whiteboard to take students on a virtual field trip. This can be a great way to explore different parts of the world, learn about historical events or visit museums and art galleries.

- Interactive story time: Use an interactive whiteboard to read and explore interactive stories. This can be a fun way to encourage reading and literacy skills while engaging students in a creative way.

14. Interactive Worksheets

Interactive worksheets are a great way to engage students and create an interactive learning experience. Here are some tips on how to create interactive worksheets for the classroom:

- Choose a topic: Choose a topic that is relevant to the curriculum and the age and reading level of your students. You can choose a math topic, a science topic, a language topic, or a social studies topic.

- Use multimedia elements: Use multimedia elements such as images, videos, and audio to enhance the learning experience. This will help to engage students and make the worksheet come alive.

- Include interactive elements: Include interactive elements such as drag and drop, clickable buttons, and interactive diagrams. This will help to keep students engaged and focused on the worksheet.

- Allow for feedback: Allow for feedback from students by including self-checking mechanisms, such as immediate feedback or a score at the end of the worksheet. This will help students to assess their own learning and reinforce what they have learned.

- Encourage creativity: Encourage creativity by allowing students to create their own interactive worksheets. This will help them to develop their technology skills and explore different learning styles.

Interactive worksheets are a great way to engage students and create an interactive learning experience. It allows students to be more involved in their learning process, encourages creativity, and helps them to retain information better.

15. Classroom Surveys

Classroom surveys can be a useful tool for teachers to gather feedback from their students and gain insights into their learning needs and preferences. Here are some tips on how to conduct effective classroom surveys:

- Identify the purpose: Identify the purpose of the survey and the questions that you want to ask. This will help you to focus the survey and ensure that you gather the information that you need.

- Use an online tool: Use an online survey tool such as Google Forms or SurveyMonkey to create and distribute your survey. These tools are easy to use and allow you to collect and analyze data quickly.

- Keep it anonymous: Encourage honesty by making the survey anonymous. This will allow students to provide honest feedback without fear of repercussions.

- Keep it short and simple: Keep the survey short and simple to encourage participation. Avoid using technical jargon and keep the questions clear and concise.

- Follow up: Follow up with students after the survey to share the results and discuss any changes that will be made based on the feedback.

Classroom surveys can be a powerful tool for teachers to gather feedback from their students and improve their teaching practices. It allows teachers to better understand the needs and preferences of their students and make adjustments to their teaching accordingly.

16. Speed Dating

Speed dating is an interactive activity that can be used in the classroom to help students get to know each other and practice communication skills. Here's how to set it up:

- Divide the class into pairs: Students are paired up and given a set amount of time to get to know each other. The length of time for each round can vary depending on the size of the class and the available time.

- Provide discussion prompts: Provide students with a list of discussion prompts or questions to guide their conversations. These prompts can be related to the curriculum, personal interests, or current events.

- Rotate the pairs: After each round of conversations, students switch partners and move to the next person. This continues until each student has had a chance to speak with every other student in the class.

- Debrief the activity: After the activity is over, take some time to debrief with the class. Ask students to share what they learned about each other and reflect on their communication skills.

Speed dating can be a fun and engaging way to help students connect with each other and practice communication skills. It can also help to create a positive and inclusive classroom environment where students feel comfortable sharing and learning from each other.

17. Picture Dictation

Picture dictation is an interactive activity that can be used to help students practice their listening and communication skills. Here's how to set it up:

- Choose a picture: Choose a picture that is relevant to the curriculum and the age and reading level of your students. This could be a diagram, a map, or an illustration.

- Pair up students: Pair up students and have one student sit with their back to the picture, while the other student has a copy of the picture.

- Give instructions: The student with the picture describes the image to their partner, who must draw it based on the instructions they are given.

- Switch roles: After a set amount of time, have students switch roles so that the other student has a chance to describe and the other to draw.

- Compare results: After the activity is over, have students compare their drawings and discuss any differences or challenges they encountered.

Picture dictation can be a fun and engaging way to help students practice their listening and communication skills. It can also help to develop their visual literacy skills and their ability to follow instructions.

18. Classroom Olympics

Classroom Olympics is a fun and engaging way to promote teamwork, cooperation, and friendly competition in the classroom. Here are some ideas for organizing a Classroom Olympics:

- Choose the events: Choose a variety of events that are age-appropriate and that can be completed in a classroom setting. Some examples might include paper airplane toss, pencil balancing relay, math challenge, and word jumble.

- Create teams: Divide the class into teams and have them choose a team name and colors. You can mix up the teams to encourage new friendships and collaboration.

- Set up the events: Set up the events around the classroom and provide instructions and materials for each one.

- Keep score: Keep score for each event and award points to the winning team. You can also award points for sportsmanship, teamwork, and creativity.

- Award medals: At the end of the Classroom Olympics, award medals to the top-performing teams and individuals. You can also provide certificates of participation for all students.

Classroom Olympics is a fun and engaging way to promote teamwork and collaboration in the classroom. It encourages healthy competition and helps students to develop a positive attitude towards learning and trying new things.

19. Classroom Jeopardy

Classroom Jeopardy is a fun and interactive game that can be used to review and reinforce concepts taught in the classroom. Here's how to set it up:

- Choose the categories: Choose categories that relate to the content covered in class. For example, if you're teaching history, you might have categories such as "Famous Battles," "Presidents," or "Civil Rights."

- Assign point values: Assign different point values to each category and level of difficulty. For example, a more difficult question might be worth 500 points, while an easier one might be worth 100 points.

- Create the questions: Create a set of questions for each category and level of difficulty. You can use the textbook or other resources to come up with questions.

- Set up the game board: Create a game board on a whiteboard or poster board with the categories and point values. Each category should have five questions with increasing point values.

- Divide the class into teams: Divide the class into teams and have each team choose a team name.

- Play the game: Have one team choose a category and point value. Read the corresponding question out loud. The first team to raise their hand gets to answer the question. If they answer correctly, they receive the corresponding point value. If they answer incorrectly, the other team gets a chance to answer.

- Keep score: Keep track of the scores on the game board and declare a winner at the end of the game.

Classroom Jeopardy is a fun and engaging way to review and reinforce concepts taught in the classroom. It encourages healthy competition and helps students to develop a positive attitude towards learning and trying new things.

20. Flashcard Games

Flashcard games are an effective way to make learning fun and engaging. Here are some ideas for flashcard games that can be used in the classroom:

- Memory Match: Place the flashcards face down on a table. Students take turns flipping over two cards at a time to try to find a matching pair. If they find a match, they keep the cards and take another turn.

- Time Race: Give each student a set of flashcards and a timer. Set a time limit and have students try to match as many cards as they can before time runs out.

- Go Fish: Give each student a set of flashcards and have them play a traditional game of Go Fish. To ask for a card, students must correctly identify the card they are requesting.

- Pictionary: Divide the class into teams and give each team a set of flashcards. Have one student from each team draw a picture of the word on the card, while the rest of the team tries to guess what it is.

- Charades: Similar to Pictionary, one student acts out the word on the flashcard while the rest of the team tries to guess what it is.

- War: Divide the class into pairs and give each pair a set of flashcards. Students flip over one card at a time and the person with the higher value card wins both cards. The player with the most cards at the end of the game wins.

Flashcard games can be adapted to fit the needs and age range of your students. They provide an opportunity for students to practice vocabulary, concepts, and skills in a fun and engaging way.

21. Cross-Classroom

Cross-classroom partnerships are a great way to foster collaboration and communication skills among students. Here are some ideas for cross-classroom partnerships:

- Pen Pal Program: Partner with a classroom in a different state or country and set up a pen pal program. Students can exchange letters, emails, or video messages to learn about each other's cultures and ways of life.

- Debate Club: Partner with another classroom and start a debate club. Students can research and prepare arguments on various topics and participate in debates with students from the other classroom.

- Buddy Reading: Partner with a lower grade classroom and set up a buddy reading program. Older students can read to younger students and help them with their reading skills.

- Science Fair: Partner with another classroom and work together to plan and execute a science fair. Students can collaborate on experiments and projects and present their findings to the rest of the school.

- Art Exchange: Partner with a classroom in a different region and set up an art exchange program. Students can create artwork and send it to the other classroom, while also receiving artwork in return.

- Language Exchange: Partner with a classroom that is learning a different language and set up a language exchange program. Students can practice speaking and writing in the language they are learning with students from the other classroom.

Cross-classroom partnerships provide students with opportunities to learn from and collaborate with others outside of their immediate community. They also promote cultural understanding and empathy, and can be a fun and rewarding experience for everyone involved.

22. Peer Evaluations

Peer evaluations can be a useful tool to help students learn and grow. Here are some ideas for peer evaluation activities:

- Group Work Evaluation: After completing a group project, have students evaluate each other's contributions. This can help students understand their strengths and weaknesses and improve their teamwork skills.

- Writing Workshop: Have students share their writing with each other and provide feedback using a peer evaluation form. This can help students develop their writing skills and learn how to give and receive constructive criticism.

- Classroom Presentations: After a student gives a presentation, have their peers evaluate them using a rubric or evaluation form. This can help students improve their public speaking skills and receive valuable feedback from their peers.

- Art Critique: Have students display their artwork and critique each other's pieces. This can help students develop their critical thinking skills and learn how to give and receive constructive feedback.

- Debate Evaluation: After a class debate, have students evaluate each other's arguments and delivery. This can help students learn how to debate effectively and improve their critical thinking skills.

Peer evaluations can help students develop their communication, critical thinking, and collaboration skills. They also provide students with valuable feedback and opportunities for growth. When implementing peer evaluations, it's important to provide clear guidelines and criteria for evaluation and encourage students to be respectful and constructive in their feedback.

23. Class Polling

Class polling is a great way to engage students in discussions and to get a sense of their opinions on various topics. Here are some ideas for class polling activities:

- Opinion Polls: Ask students to share their opinions on a particular topic, such as current events, social issues, or school policies. Use an online polling tool or ask students to raise their hands to indicate their responses. This can help promote discussion and debate in the classroom.

- Exit Polls: At the end of a class or unit, ask students to complete an exit poll to provide feedback on their learning experience. Ask questions about what they learned, what they enjoyed, and what they would like to see more of in the future.

- Quick Surveys: Use quick surveys to gather information about students' interests, learning preferences, or experiences outside of the classroom. This can help you tailor your teaching to better meet their needs.

- Quiz Show Polling: Use class polling as part of a quiz show game, where students have to answer questions on various topics. This can make learning more fun and interactive.

- Decision-Making Polls: Use class polling to make decisions about class activities or assignments. For example, ask students to vote on what book to read next, or what project to work on.

Class polling can be a useful tool to engage students and promote discussions in the classroom. It can also provide teachers with valuable insights into their students' learning experiences and interests. When implementing class polling, it's important to provide clear instructions and guidelines, and to encourage respectful and constructive participation from all students.

24. Video Analysis

Video analysis is a great way for students to develop critical thinking and analytical skills. Here are some ideas for video analysis activities:

- Film Analysis: Have students watch a film or movie and analyze its themes, character development, cinematography, and plot. Encourage them to share their insights and interpretations with the class.

- News Analysis: Have students watch a news clip or segment and analyze the way the story is presented. Ask them to identify any biases or perspectives, and to discuss how the story could be presented differently.

- Ad Analysis: Have students watch a commercial or advertisement and analyze the techniques used to persuade and market the product. Encourage them to discuss the intended audience and the effectiveness of the ad.

- Sports Analysis: Have students watch a sports game or highlight reel and analyze the strategies and techniques used by the players. Encourage them to discuss what worked well and what could be improved.

- Science Experiment Analysis: Have students watch a science experiment or demonstration and analyze the scientific principles and methods used. Encourage them to discuss the implications and potential applications of the experiment.

Video analysis can be a powerful tool for engaging students and promoting critical thinking and analytical skills. When implementing video analysis, it's important to provide clear instructions and guidelines, and to encourage students to share their insights and interpretations with the class.

25. Pair and Share

Pair and share activities are a great way for students to work together and share their ideas and insights. Here are some ideas for pair and share activities:

- Think-Pair-Share: Ask students a question or provide a prompt, and have them think individually for a few minutes. Then, pair students up and ask them to share their ideas with each other. Finally, ask a few pairs to share their ideas with the class.

- Jigsaw: Divide students into small groups and assign each group a specific topic or concept to research. Have each student in the group become an expert on one aspect of the topic, and then regroup students so that each new group has at least one expert on each topic.

- Peer Editing: Have students work in pairs to edit each other's work. Provide guidelines and a rubric to ensure that students are providing constructive feedback.

- Debate Preparation: Divide students into pairs and assign each pair a different perspective on a topic. Have them research and prepare arguments to support their perspective, and then hold a debate in class.

- Role-Playing: Assign students a scenario or situation and have them work in pairs to role-play the scenario. This can help students develop empathy and communication skills.

Pair and share activities can help students develop communication, collaboration, and critical thinking skills. When implementing pair and share activities, it's important to provide clear instructions and guidelines, and to ensure that all students have the opportunity to participate and share their ideas.

26. Think-Pair-Share Activities

Think-pair-share activities are a popular and effective way to encourage student engagement and participation. Here's how it works:

- Think: Students are given a question or prompt and are asked to think about it on their own for a few minutes. This gives them time to process the question and come up with their own ideas.

- Pair: Students are then paired up with a partner and asked to discuss their thoughts and ideas with each other. This gives them the opportunity to share their ideas with someone else and hear a different perspective.

- Share: Finally, the teacher facilitates a class discussion and invites pairs to share their thoughts and ideas with the rest of the class. This encourages students to participate and engage with their peers.

Here are some tips for implementing think-pair-share activities in your classroom:

- Make sure the question or prompt is open-ended and encourages discussion and debate.

- Give students enough time to think and pair up with a partner. This will help ensure that they have enough time to fully explore the topic.

- Encourage students to actively listen to their partner and ask follow-up questions to further the discussion.

- Facilitate a class discussion that allows for multiple perspectives and encourages students to build on each other's ideas.

- Think-pair-share activities can be used in any subject and are a great way to promote critical thinking, collaboration, and communication skills.

27. Jigsaw Activities

Jigsaw activities are a cooperative learning technique that can be used to encourage student participation and promote deeper understanding of a topic. Here's how it works:

- Divide students into groups: Divide your class into small groups of four or five students each.

- Assign topics: Assign each group a specific topic or subtopic related to the larger unit of study.

- Expert groups: Within each group, assign students to "expert groups" where they become responsible for learning about a specific aspect of the topic or subtopic.

- Research and learning: In their expert groups, students research and learn about their assigned aspect of the topic or subtopic.

- Re-group: Re-group the students into "jigsaw groups," which will include one student from each expert group. Each student in the jigsaw group shares what they learned with their group members.

- Discussion and synthesis: The jigsaw group members then discuss what they learned and synthesize the information to create a deeper understanding of the overall topic or subtopic.

Here are some tips for implementing jigsaw activities in your classroom:

- Choose a topic that is complex enough to require students to work together to create a complete understanding of it.

- Assign expert groups based on student interest or expertise to maximize engagement and participation.

- Provide students with adequate time to research and learn about their assigned aspect of the topic or subtopic.

- Encourage active listening and participation within jigsaw groups to ensure that all students contribute to the discussion and synthesis of information.

- Jigsaw activities can be used in any subject and are a great way to promote collaboration, critical thinking, and communication skills.

28. Small Group Activities

Small group activities are a great way to promote collaboration and active learning in the classroom. Here are some examples of small group activities:

- Group projects: Assigning group projects is a great way to encourage collaboration and allow students to share their skills and knowledge. Students can work together to research and present on a specific topic or create a product or prototype.

- Problem-solving tasks: Give students a problem to solve and have them work together in small groups to brainstorm solutions. This encourages critical thinking, communication, and collaboration.

- Debate or discussion groups: Assign a topic for debate or discussion and have students work in small groups to prepare their arguments or points of view. This can encourage students to explore different perspectives and communicate effectively.

- Role-playing or simulations: Have students work together in small groups to act out a scene or simulate a scenario. This can be used to teach historical events, social situations, or scientific concepts.

- Learning centers: Set up different learning centers around the classroom and have students rotate through them in small groups. This allows students to work together to explore different topics or concepts in a more hands-on and interactive way.

- Peer review or feedback groups: Have students work in small groups to provide feedback on each other's work. This can be used to improve writing skills, presentation skills, or any other skills that require constructive criticism.

When implementing small group activities in the classroom, it's important to make sure that each student has a specific role or task to complete within the group, and that each group has clear goals and objectives. Encourage active listening and communication within the groups, and provide opportunities for reflection and feedback.

29. Interactive Read-Alouds

Interactive read-alouds are a great way to engage students in a shared reading experience and promote comprehension and critical thinking skills. Here are some tips for implementing interactive read-alouds in your classroom:

- Choose the right book: Select a book that is age-appropriate and aligned with your learning objectives. Consider the book's content, themes, and illustrations, as well as the interests and reading levels of your students.

- Prepare for the read-aloud: Preview the book ahead of time and plan for interactive elements such as questions, predictions, and think-alouds. Consider using props or visual aids to enhance the reading experience.

- Model active listening and participation: Before beginning the read-aloud, model active listening and participation by explaining what you expect from your students. Encourage them to ask questions, make predictions, and share their thoughts and feelings about the story.

- Pause for discussion and reflection: Pause periodically during the read-aloud to ask questions, discuss predictions, and reflect on the story. This can help students to better understand the plot, characters, and themes of the book.

- Encourage collaboration and group work: Consider pairing students up or putting them in small groups to discuss the book and share their thoughts and ideas. This can help to build social skills and promote a sense of community in the classroom.

- Follow up with related activities: After the read-aloud, follow up with related activities such as writing prompts, art projects, or research assignments. This can help to reinforce the concepts and themes of the book and promote deeper learning.

Interactive read-alouds can be used in any subject and are a great way to promote critical thinking, language development, and a love of reading. By modeling active listening and participation and encouraging collaboration and reflection, you can help your students to become more engaged and enthusiastic readers.

30. Gallery Walks

Gallery walks are a classroom activity that involves students walking around the classroom to view and analyze various items, such as posters, artwork, or student work, that are displayed on the walls or on tables. Here are some tips for implementing gallery walks in your classroom:

- Choose the items: Select the items you want your students to view and analyze. These can be posters, artwork, student work, or any other relevant items related to your learning objectives.

- Prepare the display: Set up the items in a way that allows students to easily view and analyze them. Consider grouping the items by theme or topic, and provide information or instructions about each item.

- Give instructions: Explain to students the purpose of the gallery walk and provide instructions for what they should be doing. This might include analyzing the items, taking notes, and discussing their thoughts and ideas with classmates.

- Conduct the gallery walk: Have students walk around the classroom in small groups or pairs, viewing and analyzing each item. Encourage them to take notes and discuss their thoughts and ideas with each other.

- Debrief as a class: After the gallery walk, bring the class together for a debrief discussion. This is an opportunity for students to share their observations and insights, and to ask questions about the items they viewed.

Gallery walks are a great way to promote critical thinking, collaboration, and visual literacy skills in your students. By carefully selecting and displaying items, providing clear instructions, and facilitating a debrief discussion, you can help your students to become more engaged and thoughtful learners.

31. Picture Walks

Picture walks are a pre-reading activity that involves using illustrations to help students make predictions and generate questions about a text. Here are some tips for implementing picture walks in your classroom:

- Choose the book: Select a book that has engaging and meaningful illustrations that can be used to stimulate student interest and engagement.

- Introduce the book: Introduce the book to the students, and give a brief overview of the author, illustrator, and the genre.

- Look at the pictures: Have students examine the pictures in the book closely, asking them to describe what they see, what they think is happening in the pictures, and what questions the pictures raise.

- Make predictions: Encourage students to make predictions about the story based on what they see in the pictures. Have them share their predictions with a partner or in a small group.

- Read the book: Once students have made predictions and generated questions based on the illustrations, read the book to them. Students can then compare their predictions to what actually happens in the story.

Picture walks are a great way to get students excited about reading and to build their comprehension skills. By carefully selecting a book with engaging illustrations and facilitating a discussion of the pictures, you can help students to make predictions, generate questions, and better understand the story they are about to read.

32. KWL Charts

KWL charts are graphic organizers that help students organize their thinking and track their learning. Here are some tips for implementing KWL charts in your classroom:

- Introduce the topic: Introduce the topic or concept to be explored, and have students brainstorm what they already know about it. This can be done as a whole class or in small groups.

- Create the KWL chart: Draw a KWL chart on the board or provide a template for students to use. The chart should have three columns labeled "What We Know," "What We Want to Know," and "What We Learned."

- Fill in the "What We Know" column: Have students share what they already know about the topic and record their responses in the "What We Know" column.

- Fill in the "What We Want to Know" column: Ask students to brainstorm questions they have about the topic and record their responses in the "What We Want to Know" column.

- Conduct research: Have students conduct research to find answers to the questions they identified in the "What We Want to Know" column.

- Fill in the "What We Learned" column: After conducting research, have students share what they learned and record their responses in the "What We Learned" column.

KWL charts are a great way to activate students' prior knowledge, focus their learning, and assess their understanding. By encouraging students to ask questions, conduct research, and share their learning, KWL charts help students to take ownership of their learning and deepen their understanding of the topic at hand.

33. Exit Tickets

Exit tickets are a quick and easy way to assess student understanding at the end of a lesson or class period. Here are some tips for implementing exit tickets in your classroom:

- Determine the question: Decide on a question or prompt that will help you assess student understanding of the key concept or skill you covered in the lesson.

- Distribute the tickets: Distribute an exit ticket to each student at the end of the lesson or class period.

- Give students time to respond: Give students a few minutes to respond to the question or prompt. You may want to set a timer to keep the activity on track.

- Collect the tickets: Collect the exit tickets from students before they leave the classroom.

- Analyze the responses: Review the responses and look for patterns or common misconceptions. Use this information to guide your future lesson planning and adjust your teaching strategies to better meet student needs.

Exit tickets are a valuable tool for assessing student understanding, providing immediate feedback, and guiding future instruction. By implementing exit tickets in your classroom, you can better understand how well your students are grasping the material and adjust your teaching strategies accordingly.

34. Round-Robin Brainstorming

Round-robin brainstorming is a collaborative technique that can be used to generate ideas quickly and efficiently. Here are some tips for implementing round-robin brainstorming in your classroom:

- Define the problem or topic: Start by defining the problem or topic you want to brainstorm about. Make sure the students understand the parameters of the task and what is expected of them.

- Set the rules: Explain the rules of round-robin brainstorming to the students. This typically involves setting a time limit for each person to contribute an idea, and then moving on to the next person until everyone has had a chance to share.

- Start the brainstorming session: Begin the brainstorming session by having one student share an idea. The next student then builds on the previous idea, and so on, until all students have had a chance to contribute.

- Encourage creative thinking: Encourage students to think creatively and to build on the ideas of others. Encourage them to avoid judgment or criticism of the ideas shared.

- Record the ideas: Record the ideas on a whiteboard, poster paper, or other medium as they are shared. This will help to keep the ideas organized and visible to all students.

Round-robin brainstorming is a great way to generate a large number of ideas quickly and to encourage collaboration and creativity among students. By following these tips, you can implement this technique in your classroom and help your students to develop their critical thinking and problem-solving skills.

35. Classroom Debates

Classroom debates can be an effective way to engage students in critical thinking and help them develop their communication skills. Here are some tips for implementing classroom debates in your classroom:

- Choose a topic: Choose a topic that is relevant and interesting to your students. The topic should be open-ended enough to allow for different perspectives and arguments.

- Assign roles: Assign roles to each student, such as debater, moderator, timekeeper, or researcher.

This will help ensure that everyone has a specific task and responsibility during the debate.

- Research: Have students research their assigned topic and gather evidence to support their argument. Encourage them to use a variety of sources, including books, articles, and credible websites.

- Prepare opening statements: Have each student prepare an opening statement to present at the beginning of the debate. This should summarize their argument and key points.

- Conduct the debate: Conduct the debate using a structured format. This may involve giving each side a set amount of time to present their argument, allowing for rebuttals, and giving time for questions from the audience.

- Debrief: Debrief the debate with the students afterward. Discuss what worked well and what could be improved for future debates.

Classroom debates can be a fun and engaging way to teach critical thinking, research skills, and communication skills. By following these tips, you can implement effective debates in your classroom and help your students develop these important skills.

36. Socratic Seminars

Socratic seminars are a student-led discussion format that encourages critical thinking, collaboration, and deeper understanding of complex texts or topics. Here are some tips for implementing Socratic seminars in your classroom:

- Choose a text or topic: Choose a text or topic that is complex and open to interpretation. This can be a novel, a historical event, or a current event, for example.

- Create open-ended questions: Generate open-ended questions that encourage critical thinking and discussion. These questions should have no right or wrong answer and should prompt students to support their ideas with evidence.

- Establish ground rules: Establish clear rules for the discussion, such as taking turns speaking, active listening, and respect for diverse opinions.

- Prepare students: Prepare students for the discussion by having them read the text or research the topic in advance. Encourage them to take notes and highlight key passages.

- Conduct the discussion: Conduct the discussion using a structured format, such as the fishbowl method. This involves a small group of students sitting in a circle in the center of the room while the rest of the class observes. Students in the circle take turns answering questions and responding to each other, while the rest of the class observes and takes notes.

- Debrief: Debrief the discussion with the students afterward. Discuss what worked well and what could be improved for future Socratic seminars.

Socratic seminars can be a powerful tool for promoting critical thinking, collaboration, and deeper understanding of complex topics. By following these tips, you can implement effective Socratic seminars in your classroom and help your students develop these important skills.

37. Fishbowl Discussions

Fishbowl discussions are a structured classroom discussion technique in which a small group of students actively participate in a discussion while the rest of the class listens and observes. Here are some tips for implementing fishbowl discussions in your classroom:

- Create a small group: Choose a small group of students to participate in the fishbowl discussion. This group should be composed of students who have read and prepared for the discussion.

- Establish the rules: Before starting the discussion, establish the rules for the fishbowl. For example, set a time limit for each speaker, establish guidelines for respectful communication, and explain how students can enter and exit the discussion.

- Start the discussion: The small group of students enters the "fishbowl" area and starts the discussion. The rest of the class observes and takes notes.

- Rotate participants: After a set amount of time, rotate a few students from the observation group into the discussion group. This allows for a fresh perspective and encourages broader participation.

- Debrief the discussion: After the fishbowl discussion is over, the entire class can debrief and reflect on the discussion. Students can share their observations and insights, and the teacher can provide feedback and guidance for future discussions.

Fishbowl discussions can be an effective way to encourage deeper understanding of a topic and build students' communication and critical thinking skills. By creating a structured discussion and rotating participants, students have the opportunity to engage in a focused and productive conversation while the rest of the class learns by observing and reflecting on the discussion.

38. Chalk Talks

Chalk talks are a silent discussion technique that can be used in the classroom to engage students in meaningful dialogue around a particular topic or question. Here are some steps for implementing chalk talks in your classroom:

- Choose a topic: Select a topic or question related to your curriculum that will spark student interest and engagement.

- Set up the space: Arrange the classroom space so that students can easily see and access a large chalkboard or whiteboard.

- Write the prompt: Write the topic or question on the board in large letters, leaving plenty of space around it for students to write their ideas and thoughts.

- Silent brainstorming: Give students a set amount of time to silently brainstorm their ideas and thoughts related to the topic or question. Encourage them to use the chalkboard or whiteboard to write their ideas, comments, and questions.

- Gallery walk: After the brainstorming period is over, have students do a gallery walk to read and respond to each other's ideas and thoughts. They can use different colored chalk or markers to add their own comments and ideas to the board.

- Group discussion: Bring the class together for a group discussion of the ideas and thoughts that were shared during the chalk talk. Encourage students to build on each other's ideas and engage in respectful dialogue and debate.

Chalk talks are a great way to encourage student participation and engagement in classroom discussions. By giving students a chance to brainstorm and share their ideas in a non-verbal way, you can help them to think critically about a particular topic or question and engage in meaningful dialogue with their peers.

39. Carousel Brainstorming

Carousel brainstorming is a classroom activity that involves students working in small groups to generate and discuss ideas about a particular topic or question. Here's how to implement this activity:

- Set up the room: Arrange desks or tables in a circle or horseshoe shape. Place a large piece of paper or a whiteboard with a question or topic in the center of each table.

- Assign groups: Divide students into small groups and assign each group to a table.

- Brainstorm: Give students a set amount of time (e.g., 5-10 minutes) to brainstorm ideas about the question or topic on their table. Encourage students to write down their ideas on the paper or whiteboard.

- Rotate: After the brainstorming time is up, have each group rotate to the next table. As they move to the next table, students read the ideas generated by the previous group and add their own ideas to the list.

- Discuss: Once each group has visited all the tables, have a whole-class discussion about the ideas generated. Ask students to share the most interesting or useful ideas they saw on each table.

Carousel brainstorming is a great way to encourage collaboration and creative thinking in your classroom. It allows students to generate and build on ideas together, and it can lead to a rich and varied discussion about a particular topic or question.

40. Collaborative Writing

Collaborative writing is a process where two or more people work together to create a written document. It can be used in the classroom to help students develop their writing skills, as well as their ability to work with others. Here are some tips for implementing collaborative writing in your classroom:

- Choose a topic: Select a topic that is relevant and interesting to your students. This will help them to become more engaged in the writing process.

- Assign roles: Assign specific roles to each student, such as researcher, writer, editor, or proofreader. This will help to ensure that everyone has a specific task to complete.

- Create an outline: Have the group work together to create an outline for the writing project. This will help to ensure that everyone is on the same page and has a clear understanding of what needs to be done.

- Write in pairs or small groups: Have students work in pairs or small groups to complete different parts of the writing project. This will encourage collaboration and help students to learn from each other.

- Revise and edit: Encourage students to revise and edit each other's work. This will help them to develop their editing skills and provide feedback to their peers.

Collaborative writing can be a fun and engaging way to help students develop their writing skills while also learning how to work with others. By choosing a relevant topic, assigning roles, creating an outline, writing in pairs or small groups, and revising and editing each other's work, students can learn valuable skills that will serve them well throughout their academic and professional lives.

41. Group Research Projects

Group research projects are a great way to promote collaboration and critical thinking skills among students. Here are some steps to help you implement a successful group research project in your classroom:

- Choose a topic: Select a topic that is interesting and relevant to your students. You can choose a topic that aligns with your curriculum or let students select a topic of their choice.

- Form groups: Divide your class into small groups of 3-5 students. You can assign groups randomly or let students choose their own groups.

- Assign tasks: Assign each group member a specific task to complete, such as conducting research, taking notes, creating visuals, or writing a report.

- Provide resources: Provide students with the necessary resources to complete their research, such as books, articles, and online resources. You can also encourage students to conduct interviews or surveys to gather more information.

- Set deadlines: Set specific deadlines for each task and establish a timeline for the project. This will help students stay on track and complete the project on time.

- Monitor progress: Check in with each group regularly to monitor their progress and offer feedback. This will help students stay motivated and ensure that the project is on track.

- Present findings: Once the project is complete, have each group present their findings to the class. This will give students the opportunity to share their research and learn from their classmates.

By following these steps, you can help your students develop important research and collaboration skills while also learning about a topic that interests them.

42. Student-led Conferences

Student-led conferences are a type of conference where students take an active role in leading the discussion and sharing their learning progress with their parents or guardians. Here are some tips for implementing student-led conferences in your classroom:

- Prepare students: Before the conference, prepare students by helping them to reflect on their learning progress, set goals, and organize their work to showcase their achievements.

- Create a portfolio: Have students create a portfolio of their work to share with their parents or guardians during the conference. The portfolio should include examples of their best work, their progress towards learning goals, and reflections on their learning.

- Set the agenda: Let students take the lead in setting the agenda for the conference. Encourage them to highlight their accomplishments, share their learning goals, and discuss their strengths and areas for improvement.

- Practice: Practice with students to help them feel confident and prepared for the conference. This could include role-playing, practicing presentations, or reviewing questions they may be asked.

- Facilitate the conference: During the conference, facilitate the conversation between the student, parent or guardian, and yourself as the teacher. Encourage the student to take the lead and share their learning progress, while guiding the discussion as needed.

Student-led conferences are a powerful way to involve students in their own learning progress and to promote ownership and responsibility for their education. By preparing students, creating a portfolio, setting the agenda, practicing, and facilitating the conference, you can help students showcase their learning and feel confident in their abilities to lead a conversation about their progress.

43. Interactive Lectures

Interactive lectures are a teaching technique that combines the traditional lecture format with interactive elements to engage students in the learning process. Here are some tips for implementing interactive lectures in your classroom:

- Set clear learning objectives: Before you start your lecture, make sure you have clear learning objectives that you want your students to achieve.

- Use multimedia: Incorporate multimedia elements such as videos, images, and interactive simulations to engage students and illustrate key concepts.

- Ask questions: Encourage students to ask questions throughout the lecture to clarify understanding and promote critical thinking.

- Poll the class: Use polling software or hand-raising to gather feedback from the class and assess student comprehension.

- Small group discussions: Incorporate small group discussions or activities to allow students to apply what they have learned and engage in peer-to-peer learning.

- Summarize and review: Summarize key points at the end of the lecture and provide opportunities for students to review the material.

Interactive lectures can help students to better engage with the material and understand key concepts. By incorporating multimedia elements, asking questions, and encouraging small group discussions, you can help students to apply what they have learned and better retain the information.

44. Interactive Note-taking

Interactive note-taking is a classroom activity that encourages students to engage with course material in a meaningful way. Here are some tips for implementing interactive note-taking in your classroom:

- Provide a note-taking template: Provide students with a note-taking template that they can use to organize their notes. This might include prompts for key ideas, questions, connections, and reflections.

- Use visuals: Incorporate visuals, such as diagrams, charts, and graphs, to help students understand complex information. Encourage students to add their own visuals to their notes.

- Encourage collaboration: Encourage students to work together to create a set of shared notes. This can be done in small groups or as a class.

- Use technology: Use technology tools, such as interactive whiteboards, to facilitate note-taking. This can make note-taking more engaging and interactive.

- Use active listening strategies: Encourage students to use active listening strategies, such as asking questions, making connections, and summarizing key ideas, to help them engage with the material.

Interactive note-taking is a powerful tool for promoting active learning and helping students to better understand course material. By providing students with a note-taking template, using visuals, encouraging collaboration, using technology, and using active listening strategies, you can help students to engage with course material in a more meaningful way.

45. Interactive Feedback

Interactive feedback is a teaching approach that provides students with immediate and ongoing feedback on their learning progress. This can be done in a variety of ways, such as through class discussions, formative assessments, and peer-to-peer evaluations. Interactive feedback involves creating a collaborative learning environment where students are encouraged to ask questions, give feedback, and receive feedback from their peers and teachers. It is important for teachers to provide specific and constructive feedback to students, as this helps them understand what they are doing well and what they need to improve on.

Some examples of interactive feedback strategies include:

- Peer feedback: Students provide feedback to each other on their work. This can be done in pairs or small groups, and can be guided by rubrics or checklists.

- Teacher feedback: Teachers provide students with feedback on their work, either through written comments or one-on-one discussions.

- Formative assessments: These are assessments that are designed to provide students with feedback on their learning progress, rather than simply testing their knowledge.

- Self-assessment: Students assess their own work and provide feedback on areas where they need to improve.

Interactive feedback helps students to take ownership of their learning and to develop critical thinking and problem-solving skills. It also helps to create a positive and supportive learning environment, where students feel comfortable asking questions and seeking help.

46. One-minute Papers

One-minute papers are a quick and easy way to assess students' understanding of a lesson or topic. Here's how it works:

- At the end of a class period or lesson, ask students to take out a piece of paper and write for one minute on a specific prompt related to the lesson.

- The prompt can be something like: "What was the most important thing you learned today?" or "What question do you still have about the topic we discussed?"

- Collect the papers and quickly read through them to get a sense of how well students understood the lesson or what questions they still have.

- Use this information to guide your next lesson or to provide additional support to students who need it.

One-minute papers are a great way to quickly assess student understanding and to identify any areas where students may be struggling. They can also help students to reflect on their learning and identify questions they may have about the topic.

47. Concept Maps

Concept maps are graphical tools that help students organize and connect their knowledge about a topic or concept. They are useful for summarizing and visually representing the relationships between ideas and concepts.

To create a concept map, follow these steps:

- Choose a topic: Select a topic or concept that you want to explore.

- Identify key concepts: Write down the key concepts related to the topic. These concepts can be words or phrases that describe important ideas or themes.

- Connect concepts: Draw lines between the concepts and label the connections to show how they are related.

- Add details: Add additional details or sub-concepts to the map as needed.

- Review and revise: Review the concept map and revise it as necessary to ensure that it accurately reflects your understanding of the topic.

Concept maps can be used in a variety of ways to support learning. They can be used as a tool for brainstorming, summarizing a text, outlining a research project, or organizing notes from a lecture. By creating a visual representation of their knowledge, students can better understand and remember complex concepts.

48. Graphic Organizers

Graphic organizers are visual tools that help students organize and connect information, ideas, and concepts. There are many different types of graphic organizers, each with its own purpose and structure. Here are some examples:

- Venn diagrams: These organizers are used to compare and contrast two or more ideas, concepts, or objects. They consist of overlapping circles where the shared ideas or traits are placed in the overlapping area, while the unique ideas or traits are placed in the separate circles.

- Mind maps: These organizers help students to brainstorm and organize their ideas around a central topic or concept. They consist of a central idea or topic in the center of the map, with related subtopics and ideas branching out from it.

- Flow charts: These organizers help students to understand processes or sequences of events. They consist of boxes or shapes connected by arrows that show the flow of information or actions.

- KWL charts: These organizers help students to organize their prior knowledge, identify what they want to learn, and summarize what they have learned. They consist of three columns: "What I know," "What I want to know," and "What I learned."

- Cause-and-effect diagrams: These organizers help students to understand the relationships between events or actions. They consist of a central event or action with arrows branching out to show the causes and effects.

Graphic organizers can be used across all subject areas and grade levels to help students understand and connect complex ideas and concepts. By using visual aids to organize information, students can improve their comprehension and retention of the material.

49. Venn Diagrams

Venn diagrams are visual tools used to compare and contrast two or more things. They are typically composed of two or more overlapping circles, with each circle representing a different item or concept being compared. The overlapping sections of the circles represent the similarities between the items or concepts, while the non-overlapping sections represent their differences.

Here are some steps for creating and using a Venn diagram:

- Identify the items or concepts to be compared: Determine what you want to compare and contrast. For example, you might compare two different animals, two different books, or two different historical figures.

- Draw the circles: Draw two or more circles that overlap in the middle. Each circle should represent one of the items or concepts you are comparing.

- Label the circles: Write the name of each item or concept being compared inside its respective circle.

- Identify similarities and differences: Identify the similarities and differences between the items or concepts being compared. Write the similarities in the overlapping sections of the circles, and write the differences in the non-overlapping sections.

- Analyze the results: Use the Venn diagram to analyze the similarities and differences between the items or concepts being compared. This can help you to better understand the relationships between them.

Venn diagrams can be a useful tool for organizing information and analyzing similarities and differences between two or more items or concepts. They are commonly used in classrooms to help students compare and contrast different topics in subjects like language arts, science, and social studies.

50. Conceptual Maps

Conceptual maps are visual tools that help students to organize and represent knowledge in a hierarchical or network-like structure. They can be used to help students understand complex ideas, relationships between concepts, and to identify patterns and connections within a subject area.

Here are some tips for using conceptual maps in your classroom:

- Introduce the concept: Before creating a conceptual map, introduce the main concept or topic you want students to explore. Provide examples and clarify any unfamiliar terms or ideas.

- Brainstorm ideas: Ask students to brainstorm ideas related to the concept and write them down.

These can be individual or group brainstorming sessions.

- Organize ideas: Once students have generated a list of ideas, have them organize the ideas into categories or subtopics. Encourage students to think about how the ideas are related to each other.

- Create the map: Using a whiteboard or graphic organizer software, have students create a visual representation of the concept and its related ideas. Use arrows or lines to show connections between ideas.

- Review and revise: Once the map is complete, review it as a class and have students discuss any areas of confusion or disagreement. Encourage students to revise the map as needed to reflect their understanding of the concept.

Conceptual maps can be used in any subject area and at any grade level. They are a powerful tool for promoting critical thinking, understanding complex concepts, and encouraging student creativity.

51. Brain Maps

Brain maps, also known as mind maps, are visual diagrams that are used to organize and connect ideas, concepts, and information. They are a type of graphic organizer that can be used to help students better understand and remember information, as well as to develop critical thinking skills. To create a brain map, start with a central idea or topic and branch out from there, adding related subtopics and connecting them with lines. Use keywords, images, and symbols to help make connections between ideas and concepts. Brain maps can be created on paper, whiteboards, or with specialized software.

Here are some tips for using brain maps in the classroom:

- Brainstorming: Use brain maps to help students brainstorm and organize their ideas for writing assignments or projects.

- Note-taking: Use brain maps to help students take notes during lectures or while reading, organizing key concepts and ideas in a visual way.

- Vocabulary: Use brain maps to help students learn new vocabulary words, making connections between related words and concepts.

- Problem-solving: Use brain maps to help students solve complex problems, breaking down the problem into smaller components and visualizing possible solutions.

- Review: Use brain maps to help students review and remember information, summarizing key concepts and connections in a visual format.

Brain maps are a powerful tool for helping students to organize, connect, and remember information. They can be used in a variety of subjects and settings, and are a great way to engage students in the learning process.

52. Frayer Models

Frayer models are graphic organizers used to help students learn new concepts and vocabulary. They typically consist of a four-box grid with the word or concept being studied in the middle box, and the other boxes used for definitions, examples, and non-examples.

Here's how to use a Frayer model:

- Introduce the word or concept: Start by writing the word or concept in the middle box of the Frayer model.

- Provide a definition: Have students brainstorm a definition for the word or concept and write it in one of the surrounding boxes.

- Give examples: Students can then list examples of the word or concept in another surrounding box. These can be drawn from personal experience or from a text.

- Identify non-examples: Finally, students should identify non-examples of the word or concept in the remaining box. These are things that do not fit the definition of the word or concept.

By using a Frayer model, students are able to engage with new concepts in a visual and interactive way. The model encourages students to think deeply about the meaning of a word or concept and how it can be applied in different contexts.

53. Interactive Storytelling

Interactive storytelling is an engaging and effective way to teach important concepts, build literacy skills, and encourage creativity in students. Here are some tips for implementing interactive storytelling in your classroom:

- Choose a story: Choose a story that is appropriate for your students' age and interests. Look for stories that have a strong narrative structure and engaging characters.

- Get students involved: Encourage students to actively participate in the storytelling process. Ask them to create sound effects, act out parts of the story, or even contribute to the plot.

- Use props: Props can help to make the story come alive and engage students' senses. Use simple props such as hats, scarves, or stuffed animals to represent characters or objects in the story.

- Ask questions: Ask questions throughout the storytelling process to encourage students to think critically about the story. Ask them to make predictions about what will happen next or to analyze characters' motivations and actions.

- Encourage creativity: Interactive storytelling is a great opportunity to encourage creativity in students. Encourage them to create their own stories or to modify the existing story to create new endings or characters.

Interactive storytelling is a fun and effective way to engage students in learning and help them develop important literacy and critical thinking skills. By choosing engaging stories, encouraging student participation, using props, asking questions, and encouraging creativity, you can make interactive storytelling a valuable part of your classroom.

54. Interactive Simulations

Interactive simulations are a type of learning activity that allow students to explore complex concepts and systems in a virtual environment. Simulations can be used to create a realistic representation of a real-world situation, or to simulate the behavior of a system or process.

There are many benefits to using interactive simulations in the classroom, including:

- Engagement: Simulations can be fun and engaging, which can help to motivate students to learn and to stay focused on the task at hand.

- Active learning: Simulations require students to actively participate in the learning process, rather than simply listening to a lecture or reading a textbook.

- Immediate feedback: Simulations can provide immediate feedback to students, allowing them to learn from their mistakes and to make adjustments to their approach.

- Exploration: Simulations allow students to explore complex concepts and systems in a safe and controlled environment, without the risk of real-world consequences.

- Accessibility: Simulations can be accessed from anywhere, which makes them ideal for remote learning or for students who are unable to attend class in person.

Some examples of interactive simulations include virtual labs for science classes, interactive simulations for math and physics, and simulations for learning about historical events or cultural phenomena. These simulations can be found online, or can be created by teachers using software or other tools.

55. Role-playing Games

Role-playing games (RPGs) are interactive classroom activities that involve students taking on roles of characters and acting out scenarios or situations. In an educational setting, RPGs can be used to teach a variety of subjects, such as history, literature, social studies, or even science.

To implement a role-playing game in your classroom, follow these steps:

- Choose a scenario: Select a scenario that aligns with the learning objectives of your lesson. For example, if you are teaching about the American Revolution, you might create a scenario where students take on the roles of American colonists and British soldiers during a battle.

- Assign roles: Assign roles to each student, and provide them with a brief description of their character and their motivations. Encourage students to think about how their character fits into the scenario and how they can act in character to achieve their goals.

- Set the scene: Provide a brief overview of the setting and the situation to the students, and set the scene for the role-playing activity.

- Act out the scenario: Have students act out the scenario by interacting with one another and making decisions based on their character's motivations and objectives.

- Debrief: After the role-playing activity is complete, debrief with the students to discuss what they learned and how the activity connects to the lesson objectives.

By using RPGs in your classroom, you can help students develop their creativity, critical thinking skills, and empathy. Additionally, it can provide an engaging and fun way for students to learn and connect with the material.

56. Drama Performances

Drama performances are a great way to engage students and enhance their communication and collaboration skills. Here are some tips for implementing drama performances in your classroom:

- Choose a script or create your own: Choose a script that is appropriate for your students' age and level, or work with them to create their own script.

- Assign roles: Assign roles to students based on their interests and strengths. Make sure to include both major and minor roles to ensure everyone has a chance to participate.

- Rehearse: Set aside time for students to rehearse their lines and practice their scenes. Encourage them to work collaboratively and give feedback to one another.

- Decorate the stage: Work with students to create or decorate the stage to enhance the performance. This can include creating props, scenery, or costumes.

- Perform: Invite an audience to watch the performance. This can be parents, other classes, or school staff. Encourage students to take ownership of the performance and feel proud of their hard work.

Drama performances can be a fun and engaging way to teach important skills such as teamwork, communication, and creativity. By providing students with a platform to express themselves and work collaboratively, they can develop their confidence and improve their overall academic performance.

57. Mystery Games

Mystery games are a fun and engaging way to promote critical thinking, problem-solving, and collaboration skills in the classroom. In a mystery game, students work together to solve a fictional crime by gathering clues, analyzing evidence, and using deductive reasoning to identify the culprit.

To implement a mystery game in your classroom, follow these steps:

- Choose a mystery story: Select a mystery story that is appropriate for your students' age and reading level. You can either create your own story or use a pre-existing one.

- Set the scene: Introduce the story and set the scene for the crime. Explain the background of the crime, the setting, and the characters involved.

- Provide clues: Give students a set of clues that they can use to solve the mystery. Clues can be presented in various formats such as written notes, physical objects, or even video clips.

- Analyze evidence: Encourage students to analyze the clues and evidence to come up with theories about what happened.

- Solve the mystery: As students work together to solve the mystery, encourage them to use critical thinking, problem-solving, and collaboration skills to identify the culprit.

- Debrief: After the mystery is solved, debrief with the students to discuss their thought process, the clues they found most helpful, and how they worked together to solve the crime.

Mystery games can be a great way to promote collaboration, problem-solving, and critical thinking skills in your classroom. By using fictional crimes to engage your students' curiosity, you can help them to develop the skills they need to succeed both in and out of the classroom.

58. Escape Room Activities

Escape room activities are interactive games that can be used in the classroom to engage students in problem-solving, critical thinking, and teamwork. Here are some tips for implementing escape room activities in your classroom:

- Choose a theme: Choose a theme for your escape room that is relevant and engaging to your students. It could be based on a historical event, a science concept, or a literature topic.

- Create a storyline: Create a storyline that will guide the players through the escape room. The storyline should be engaging and challenging, with a clear objective and a set of clues to help the players solve the puzzle.

- Set up the room: Set up the room with puzzles, riddles, and clues that the players will need to solve to escape. You can use a combination of physical puzzles and digital puzzles to make the game more engaging.

- Divide the class into teams: Divide the class into teams of 3-5 players. Each team should have a designated team leader to keep the team organized and on track.

- Set a time limit: Set a time limit for the escape room activity. Typically, escape rooms last between 30 minutes and one hour.

- Debrief: Once the escape room activity is over, debrief with the class. Discuss the clues, the puzzles, and the teamwork that went into solving the mystery.

Escape room activities can be a fun and engaging way to reinforce learning and build critical thinking skills. With a little creativity and planning, you can create an escape room activity that is tailored to the needs and interests of your students.

59. Breakout Sessions

Breakout sessions are small group discussions or activities that take place within a larger group or meeting. They are designed to provide participants with an opportunity to engage in deeper and more focused conversations around a particular topic, idea, or question.

Here are some tips for facilitating breakout sessions:

- Define the purpose: Clearly define the purpose of the breakout session and communicate it to the participants. This will help them understand the objective of the discussion and stay focused.

- Provide clear instructions: Provide clear instructions to the participants about the task or activity they will be engaging in during the breakout session. Make sure they understand the rules and expectations.

- Assign roles: Assign roles within the breakout groups to ensure that everyone has a task to complete and a voice in the discussion. This will help to keep everyone engaged and prevent any one person from dominating the conversation.

- Set a time limit: Set a time limit for the breakout session and make sure everyone is aware of it. This will help to keep the conversation focused and prevent it from running over time.

- Debrief: Once the breakout session is over, bring everyone back together and ask each group to share their key takeaways or insights. This will help to consolidate the learning and ensure that everyone benefits from the discussion.

Breakout sessions are a great way to promote collaboration and engagement within a larger group setting. By providing participants with an opportunity to engage in focused and meaningful discussions, you can help to deepen their understanding of a particular topic or idea and encourage them to share their insights and perspectives with others.

60. Critical Thinking Games

Critical thinking games are designed to promote and develop students' ability to analyze and evaluate information and ideas in order to make reasoned judgments and decisions. Here are some examples of critical thinking games that can be used in the classroom:

- The Socratic Game: In this game, students take turns presenting a statement or question, and the rest of the class must ask questions to clarify and challenge the statement or question until they reach a deeper understanding of the topic.

- Clue: This classic board game challenges players to use logic and reasoning to solve a murder mystery.

- Brain Teasers: Brain teasers are puzzles or riddles that require critical thinking and problem-solving skills to solve.

- Code Breaking Games: These games involve decoding secret messages and require logical and analytical thinking to decipher the code.

- Board Games: Many board games, such as chess or Settlers of Catan, require strategic thinking and decision-making skills.

- Debate Games: Debate games challenge students to develop persuasive arguments and to think critically about their opponent's position.

- Logic Puzzles: Logic puzzles, such as Sudoku or Minesweeper, require critical thinking and problem-solving skills to complete.

- Word Games: Word games, such as Scrabble or Bananagrams, require players to think creatively and strategically to form words and score points.

These games can be a fun and engaging way to help students develop their critical thinking skills, while also building teamwork and collaboration skills.

61. Decision-making Games

Decision-making games are interactive activities that allow students to practice making decisions in a safe and fun environment. These games can be used to teach critical thinking skills, problem-solving skills, and decision-making skills. Here are some examples of decision-making games that you can use in your classroom:

- The Price is Right: In this game, students are given a set of products and asked to guess the price of each item. This game helps students to think critically about the value of products and the factors that influence their price.

- Risk Management Game: In this game, students are given a set of scenarios and asked to identify potential risks and develop strategies to manage them. This game helps students to think critically about risk assessment and risk management.

- The Stock Market Game: In this game, students are given a set amount of money to invest in the stock market. This game helps students to think critically about the factors that influence the stock market and how to make informed investment decisions.

- Game of Life: In this game, students are given a set of scenarios that they must navigate, such as choosing a career, buying a house, and starting a family. This game helps students to think critically about the decisions they make and the consequences of those decisions.

- Oregon Trail: In this game, students must navigate a wagon train from Missouri to Oregon in the 19th century. This game helps students to think critically about the challenges of traveling long distances and making decisions in uncertain environments.

Using decision-making games in the classroom can help students to develop critical thinking skills, problem-solving skills, and decision-making skills. These games provide a fun and interactive way for students to learn important life skills that will serve them well in the future.

62. Business Simulations

Business simulations are interactive learning tools designed to simulate real-world business scenarios and allow students to develop and apply their knowledge and skills in a risk-free environment. Here are some tips for implementing business simulations in your classroom:

- Choose the right simulation: Select a simulation that aligns with your learning objectives and that is appropriate for your students' age and skill level.

- Provide context: Introduce the simulation by providing context and background information about the industry, market, and business environment in which the simulation is set.

- Set objectives: Clearly define the learning objectives for the simulation, and provide students with specific tasks and goals to achieve.

- Provide guidance: Provide students with guidance and support throughout the simulation, including resources, tools, and feedback.

- Debrief and reflect: After the simulation, debrief with students and encourage them to reflect on what they learned, what worked well, and what could be improved.

Business simulations are an engaging and effective way to teach students about various aspects of business, including marketing, finance, and management. By immersing students in realistic business scenarios, simulations can help them develop critical thinking, problem-solving, and decision-making skills that are applicable in a variety of real-world contexts.

63. Classroom Simulations

Classroom simulations are a type of interactive learning activity that allows students to simulate real-world situations or scenarios in a controlled classroom environment. These simulations can be designed to teach a variety of subjects and concepts, including history, science, economics, and more.

Here are some tips for implementing classroom simulations:

- Choose a relevant topic: Choose a topic that is relevant to your curriculum and that will engage your students. For example, you could simulate a historical event, a scientific experiment, or a business scenario.

- Provide clear instructions: Clearly explain the rules of the simulation and the objectives that students are expected to achieve.

- Assign roles: Assign each student a specific role to play in the simulation, and provide them with the necessary information and resources to fulfill their role.

- Encourage collaboration: Encourage students to work together and to share information and resources to achieve their objectives.

- Debrief: After the simulation is over, debrief with your students to discuss what they learned, what worked well, and what could be improved in future simulations.

Classroom simulations can be a fun and engaging way to teach complex concepts and to help students develop critical thinking, problem-solving, and collaboration skills. By carefully designing the simulation and providing clear instructions, you can create a meaningful and memorable learning experience for your students.

64. Classroom Trials

Classroom trials are a type of classroom activity that simulates a court trial in which students take on roles of lawyers, witnesses, and jurors to explore issues related to law, justice, and critical thinking. Here are some tips for implementing a classroom trial:

- Choose a case: Choose a case that is age-appropriate, interesting, and relevant to the students. You can find cases related to social issues, historical events, or literary works.

- Assign roles: Assign roles to students, including lawyers, witnesses, and jurors. Students can work in groups or individually, depending on the case and the size of the class.

- Research and preparation: Students should research and prepare their arguments and evidence to present during the trial. They can use primary and secondary sources, such as court documents, witness statements, and expert opinions.

- Conduct the trial: Students should present their opening and closing statements, examine and cross-examine witnesses, and present evidence to support their case. The teacher can act as a judge or appoint a student to act as a judge.

- Reflect and evaluate: After the trial, students should reflect on their performance and evaluate their strengths and weaknesses. The teacher can facilitate a discussion on the issues related to law, justice, and critical thinking.

Classroom trials can be a fun and engaging way to teach critical thinking, public speaking, and collaboration skills. By immersing students in a simulated courtroom, they can learn about the legal system, develop empathy for different perspectives, and explore complex issues.

65. Debate Tournaments

Debate tournaments are a great way to engage students in critical thinking, research, and public speaking skills. Here are some tips for organizing a successful debate tournament in your classroom:

- Choose a topic: Select a topic that is relevant, interesting, and appropriate for your students' age and maturity level. Encourage students to research and prepare arguments on both sides of the issue.

- Form teams: Divide students into teams of two or three, and assign each team a side of the argument. Encourage students to work together to develop strong arguments and evidence to support their position.

- Establish rules and procedures: Set clear rules and procedures for the debate, including time limits for each speaker, guidelines for rebuttals, and procedures for addressing questions from the audience.

- Schedule the debate: Set a date and time for the debate, and create a schedule that allows time for opening statements, rebuttals, and closing arguments.

- Invite judges: Invite a panel of judges to evaluate the debate and provide feedback to the students. Consider inviting community members, teachers, or other experts in the field to serve as judges.

- Prepare students: Provide students with guidance and support as they prepare for the debate. Encourage them to practice their arguments and work on their public speaking skills.

- Hold the debate: On the day of the debate, create a supportive and respectful environment for students to present their arguments. Encourage the audience to ask questions and engage in thoughtful discussion.

Debate tournaments can be a fun and engaging way to teach critical thinking, research, and public speaking skills. By providing guidance and support, and creating a supportive environment, you can help students develop these important skills and build their confidence as speakers and thinkers.

66. Spelling Bees

A spelling bee is a competition in which participants are asked to spell a broad selection of words, usually with a varying degree of difficulty. Spelling bees can be held in a classroom or school setting, as well as at the regional, national, or international level.

To organize a spelling bee in the classroom, the following steps can be taken:

- Set up guidelines: Establish guidelines for the spelling bee, including eligibility criteria, rules, and format.

- Choose words: Select words for the spelling bee that are appropriate for the grade level and that students are expected to know.

- Conduct a practice round: Conduct a practice round with the class to explain the format and rules of the spelling bee.

- Begin the competition: Begin the competition by calling out the name of the first participant and a word to be spelled. If the participant spells the word correctly, they proceed to the next round. If they spell the word incorrectly, they are eliminated from the competition.

- Determine the winner: Continue with the competition until only one participant is left, who is declared the winner.

Spelling bees are not only a fun way to engage students in spelling but also an opportunity to improve their spelling and vocabulary skills. It can also help boost their confidence and promote healthy competition among students.

67. Poetry Slams

Poetry slams are a type of competitive poetry reading where participants perform their original works in front of an audience and a panel of judges. Here are some tips for organizing a poetry slam in your classroom:

- Introduce poetry: Introduce your students to different forms of poetry and encourage them to read and write their own poems.

- Explain the slam: Explain to your students what a poetry slam is and how it works. Discuss the rules and judging criteria with them.

- Set the stage: Set up a stage or performance area in your classroom, and make sure there is seating for your audience.

- Recruit judges: Recruit judges for the slam. They can be teachers, students, or community members.

- Select participants: Have students sign up to participate in the slam. You can limit the number of participants to keep the event manageable.

- Practice sessions: Host practice sessions where students can perform their poems and receive feedback from their peers.

- Run the slam: On the day of the slam, have each participant perform their poem in front of the audience and judges. After all the poems have been read, the judges will announce the winner.

Poetry slams are a fun and creative way to get students engaged with poetry and encourage them to express themselves through writing and performance. By providing opportunities for students to practice and receive feedback, you can help them build their confidence and develop their skills as writers and performers.

68. Writing Competitions

Writing competitions are a great way to encourage students to develop their writing skills while also fostering creativity and self-expression. Here are some tips for organizing a writing competition in your classroom:

- Choose the type of competition: There are many different types of writing competitions, such as essay contests, poetry contests, short story contests, and more. Choose the type of competition that best fits the interests and abilities of your students.

- Establish the rules: Clearly define the rules and guidelines for the competition, including the topic, word count, and submission deadline. Also, provide guidelines for judging the entries.

- Create a scoring rubric: Develop a scoring rubric that outlines the criteria for judging the entries. Make sure the rubric is clear and concise and provides specific criteria for evaluating the entries.

- Set up prizes: Decide on the prizes for the winners. Consider providing a certificate of recognition, a book, or a small gift certificate.

- Promote the competition: Advertise the competition to your students and encourage them to participate. Post the rules, guidelines, and scoring rubric in a visible location in your classroom.

- Judge the entries: Once the deadline for submissions has passed, review and score the entries using the scoring rubric. Consider enlisting the help of other teachers or even parents to assist with judging.

- Announce the winners: Hold an awards ceremony to announce the winners and award the prizes. Consider publishing the winning entries in a school newsletter or on a bulletin board to showcase the talent of your students.

A writing competition can be a fun and engaging way to motivate students to develop their writing skills and express themselves creatively. With careful planning, clear guidelines, and thoughtful judging, you can create a successful writing competition in your classroom.

69. Presentation Competitions

Presentation competitions can be an excellent way to motivate students to develop their public speaking skills while also showcasing their knowledge on a particular topic. Here are some tips for organizing a successful presentation competition:

- Choose the format: Decide on the format of the competition, such as individual or group presentations, and establish guidelines for the length of presentations, visual aids, and other requirements.

- Select the topic: Choose a relevant and engaging topic that will encourage students to do research and prepare well-crafted presentations. You can also consider allowing students to select their own topics, within certain guidelines.

- Set the judging criteria: Establish clear and objective judging criteria, such as organization, content, delivery, and visual aids. Provide a rubric to the judges to ensure consistency in the evaluation process.

- Invite judges: Recruit judges who are knowledgeable about the topic and experienced in public speaking. Consider inviting community members, parents, or other teachers to serve as judges.

- Provide training: Offer training sessions or workshops to help students develop their presentation skills and prepare for the competition.

- Host the competition: Set a date and location for the competition and invite participants, judges, and audience members. Encourage the audience to participate by asking questions or providing feedback to the presenters.

- Award prizes: Recognize the top performers with certificates, trophies, or other prizes. Consider awarding prizes for categories such as best individual presentation, best group presentation, and most creative use of visual aids.

A presentation competition can be a fun and rewarding experience for both students and teachers. By providing students with the opportunity to showcase their knowledge and skills, you can help them develop their confidence and become more effective communicators.

70. Science Fairs

Science fairs are events where students showcase their science projects to judges and the public. These events provide students with an opportunity to display their knowledge and creativity in the field of science. Here are some tips for organizing a science fair:

- Choose a date: Choose a date that is suitable for students, teachers, and judges. Consider holidays and other school events.

- Create a theme: Choose a theme for the science fair that can be related to the curriculum or current events.

- Invite participants: Invite students to participate in the science fair. Provide guidelines and timelines for submitting projects.

- Choose judges: Choose judges who have experience in science and are capable of evaluating the projects.

- Provide resources: Provide students with resources such as books, journals, and websites to help them with their projects.

- Arrange for space: Arrange for a space that is suitable for displaying the projects. This could be a gym, cafeteria, or classroom.

- Set up the projects: Set up the projects on the day of the science fair. Ensure that there is enough space for students to move around and that the projects are clearly labeled.

- Judging: Conduct the judging process. Judges should evaluate the projects based on criteria such as creativity, scientific method, and presentation.

- Award ceremony: Hold an award ceremony to recognize the students who have excelled in their projects. Provide certificates or prizes for the winners.

Science fairs are an excellent way to encourage students to develop an interest in science and to showcase their talents. By organizing a science fair, you can provide students with an opportunity to learn, be creative, and engage in scientific inquiry.

71. Cultural Fairs

Cultural fairs are events that showcase the diversity of cultures represented in a school or community. These events can be a great way to celebrate and learn about different cultures and promote multicultural understanding and awareness.

Here are some ideas for organizing a cultural fair:

- Planning: Start by forming a committee of teachers, parents, and students to plan the fair. Decide on the theme and date of the fair, and assign tasks to committee members.

- Participants: Reach out to members of the school or community who are interested in sharing their culture at the fair. This can include families, community groups, and local businesses.

- Booths: Each participant should be assigned a booth to showcase their culture. Booths can include food, music, dance, art, and crafts. Encourage participants to provide interactive and educational displays to engage visitors.

- Performances: Plan a schedule of performances that showcase different cultures. This can include dance, music, poetry, and storytelling.

- Activities: Provide activities that allow visitors to participate and learn about different cultures. This can include cultural games, crafts, and cooking demonstrations.

- Promotion: Promote the fair through school and community channels, such as social media, flyers, and newsletters.

- A cultural fair is a great way to bring together the diverse members of a school or community and celebrate the unique cultural contributions of each group.

72. Interactive Exhibits

Interactive exhibits are a great way to engage students in hands-on learning experiences that help to reinforce key concepts and promote deeper understanding. Here are some tips for implementing an interactive exhibits activity in your classroom:

- Choose a topic: Select a topic that aligns with your curriculum and standards, and that you think will engage your students.

- Develop your exhibits: Create a set of interactive exhibits that allow students to explore key concepts related to your topic. Each exhibit should be hands-on and engaging, and should include a clear learning objective.

- Set up your exhibits: Set up your exhibits around the classroom, ensuring that each exhibit has enough space for students to explore and interact with it.

- Introduce the activity: Introduce the interactive exhibits activity to your students, explaining the purpose of the activity and how it aligns with your curriculum and learning objectives.

- Rotate through the exhibits: Divide your students into small groups and have them rotate through each of the exhibits, spending a set amount of time at each one.

- Facilitate discussion: After students have had a chance to explore each exhibit, bring the class together for a group discussion. Encourage students to share what they learned and how the exhibits helped to reinforce key concepts.

Interactive exhibits activities are a fun and engaging way to promote hands-on learning and reinforce key concepts. By carefully selecting a topic and developing interactive exhibits that align with your curriculum and learning objectives, you can create a memorable and effective learning experience for your students.

73. Interactive Art Projects

Interactive art projects are hands-on activities that allow students to engage with art in a creative way. These projects can be used to build students' art skills, spark creativity, and promote teamwork. Here are some ideas for interactive art projects:

- Collaborative murals: Divide students into small groups and have each group create a section of a mural on a large sheet of paper or canvas. When the individual sections are complete, combine them to create a larger piece of artwork.

- Graffiti walls: Create a temporary graffiti wall in the classroom or schoolyard using paper or a chalkboard. Students can draw and write messages on the wall, expressing their ideas and creativity.

- Found object sculptures: Collect a variety of objects (such as bottle caps, old toys, or scraps of fabric) and ask students to create sculptures using these materials. Encourage them to think outside the box and experiment with different combinations of objects.

- Collaborative installations: Have students work together to create a large-scale installation using materials such as fabric, paper, or cardboard. This can be displayed in the classroom or schoolyard for others to enjoy.

- Interactive drawing games: Set up a drawing game where one student starts by drawing a small picture or pattern, then passes the paper to another student who adds to the drawing. Continue passing the paper around until the drawing is complete.

Interactive art projects are a fun and engaging way to explore art and creativity. By working together and experimenting with different materials and techniques, students can develop their artistic skills and express their ideas in new and exciting ways.

74. Interactive Music Projects

Interactive music projects are activities that allow students to engage with music in a hands-on way, promoting creativity, critical thinking, and musical skill development. Here are some examples of interactive music projects:

- Songwriting: Students can write their own songs, either individually or in groups. This activity involves coming up with lyrics, melody, and harmony, and can be done with any genre of music.

- Music production: Students can learn to use digital audio workstations (DAWs) and other music production software to create and record their own music. This can include recording live instruments or vocals, sampling, and mixing.

- Instrument building: Students can build their own musical instruments using recycled materials or other simple materials. This activity allows students to explore the physics of sound and develop their creativity.

- Soundscapes: Students can create soundscapes by recording and manipulating different sounds, such as nature sounds or city sounds. This activity promotes active listening and sound design skills.

- Music videos: Students can create music videos to accompany their own songs or existing songs. This activity allows students to explore the visual aspect of music and develop their storytelling skills.

Interactive music projects can be adapted for students of all ages and skill levels, and can be used to teach a variety of musical concepts and skills. These projects can also be integrated into other subjects, such as language arts or social studies, to create interdisciplinary learning experiences.

75. Interactive Dance Projects

Interactive dance projects are a great way to engage students in physical activity while also promoting creativity and self-expression. Here are some tips for implementing interactive dance projects in your classroom:

- Choose a theme or concept: Start by choosing a theme or concept for the dance project, such as a specific style of dance or a particular piece of music.

- Provide examples: Show students examples of different types of dance or specific dance moves related to the chosen theme or concept. You can use videos, pictures, or demonstrations to help students understand the movements and techniques involved.

- Practice and rehearse: Allow students to practice and rehearse their dance routines. Encourage them to experiment with different movements and to work collaboratively to develop a cohesive performance.

- Share and perform: Once the dance routines are complete, provide opportunities for students to share and perform their dances for an audience. This can be in front of the class, in a school assembly, or even virtually.

- Reflect and evaluate: After the performance, facilitate a reflection and evaluation session where students can discuss what they learned, what they enjoyed, and what they would do differently next time.

Interactive dance projects can be a fun and engaging way to promote physical activity, creativity, and collaboration in the classroom. By choosing a theme or concept, providing examples, practicing and rehearsing, and sharing and performing, students can develop their dance skills and build their confidence in performing in front of others.

76. Interactive Drama Projects

Interactive drama projects involve students in creating and performing a play or skit in which they explore different themes or topics. Here are some tips for implementing interactive drama projects in your classroom:

- Choose a topic: Select a theme or topic that is relevant and interesting to your students. It could be a social issue, a historical event, or a piece of literature.

- Research: Have students research the topic to gain a deeper understanding and to gather ideas for their play. Encourage them to use a variety of sources, such as books, articles, and videos.

- Create a script: Once students have researched the topic, have them work in groups to create a script for their play. Encourage them to use their creativity and imagination, and to incorporate different perspectives and viewpoints.

- Rehearse: After the script is complete, have students rehearse their play, practicing their lines, blocking, and character development.

- Perform: Once students have rehearsed their play, have them perform it for the class or for an audience outside of the classroom.

Interactive drama projects can be a powerful way to engage students in learning and to help them develop important skills such as collaboration, critical thinking, and communication. By working together to create and perform a play, students can explore complex issues and develop a deeper understanding of the world around them.

77. Interactive Media Projects

Interactive media projects involve the use of technology to create engaging and interactive learning experiences. Here are some examples:

- Digital storytelling: Students can use multimedia tools like video editing software or online platforms to create their own stories that incorporate text, images, video, and audio.

- Podcasts: Students can research, write, and record their own podcasts on topics related to the curriculum. They can interview experts, share their own perspectives, and present their findings to their peers.

- Virtual field trips: Students can explore places and cultures around the world using virtual reality or augmented reality tools. They can visit museums, historical sites, or natural landmarks, and interact with the environment in a way that would not be possible in real life.

- Video games: Students can design and create their own video games that incorporate elements of the curriculum. They can learn coding and game design skills, while also engaging with content in a new and exciting way.

- Interactive websites: Students can use website builders or coding tools to create their own websites that showcase their learning. They can share their research, writing, or multimedia projects, and include interactive elements like quizzes, polls, or videos.

Interactive media projects offer students the opportunity to explore content in a dynamic and engaging way. By incorporating technology into the learning process, students can develop digital literacy skills, creativity, and critical thinking.

78. Interactive Book Clubs

Interactive book clubs are a great way to encourage students to read and engage with literature while promoting critical thinking and discussion skills. Here are some tips for implementing interactive book clubs in your classroom:

- Choose a book: Select a book that is appropriate for the age and reading level of your students, and that will be of interest to them. Consider books that deal with themes or issues relevant to your curriculum or that tie into current events.

- Divide students into groups: Divide students into small groups of 4-6 and assign each group a portion of the book to read. You can either assign chapters or sections of the book or have students self-select the section they would like to read.

- Assign roles: Assign each student in the group a role, such as discussion leader, summarizer, connector, or word wizard. Each role has a specific responsibility during the book club meetings.

- Set a schedule: Set a schedule for the book club meetings, with each meeting focusing on a different portion of the book. Make sure to give students enough time to read the assigned section before each meeting.

- Hold meetings: During the book club meetings, have students discuss their assigned section, focusing on the themes, characters, and events of the book. Encourage students to share their thoughts, ask questions, and make connections to their own lives.

- Wrap-up: After all of the book club meetings are completed, hold a wrap-up session where students can discuss the book as a whole. Encourage students to share their favorite parts of the book, what they learned, and how the book made them feel.

Interactive book clubs are a great way to encourage students to read and engage with literature, while also promoting critical thinking and discussion skills. By dividing students into small groups, assigning roles, and setting a schedule, you can help ensure that students are actively engaged in the reading process and are getting the most out of their reading experience.

79. Classroom Book Clubs

Classroom book clubs are a fun and engaging way to promote reading comprehension and critical thinking skills among students. Here are some tips for implementing successful classroom book clubs:

- Choose appropriate books: Select books that are appropriate for the grade level and reading level of the students. Choose books that are interesting, engaging, and relevant to the students' interests.

- Form book club groups: Divide students into small groups of 4-6 students, and assign each group a book to read.

- Schedule regular meetings: Schedule regular book club meetings, either during class time or after school. Encourage students to set goals and deadlines for completing the book.

- Facilitate discussions: Provide students with discussion questions or prompts to help guide their conversations during book club meetings. Encourage students to share their thoughts and opinions, ask questions, and listen to their peers.

- Encourage collaboration: Encourage students to work together to analyze and interpret the book. Students can take turns leading the discussion or presenting their findings to the group.

- Promote critical thinking: Encourage students to think critically about the book, its themes, and its characters. Encourage students to make connections to their own lives and experiences.

- Assess learning: Assess students' learning by having them write a book review or give a presentation on the book. Encourage students to use evidence from the book to support their arguments.

By implementing classroom book clubs, you can promote a love of reading, build critical thinking skills, and foster a sense of community and collaboration in your classroom.

80. Book Exchange Activities

Book exchange activities are a fun and engaging way to encourage students to read and share their love of books. Here are some ideas for book exchange activities:

- Book Swap: Organize a book swap where students bring in books they have already read and exchange them with others in the class. This can be a great way for students to discover new authors and genres.

- Blind Date with a Book: Wrap books in brown paper or other materials to keep the title and cover hidden. Label them with short descriptions or keywords to give a hint about the content. Students can choose a book based on the description and unwrap it to reveal their "date."

- Book Recommendation Board: Create a bulletin board where students can post short book reviews and recommendations for others in the class. This can be a great way to get students excited about reading and to discover new books and authors.

- Book Club: Start a book club in the classroom where students can read and discuss books together. This can be a great way to encourage critical thinking and engage students in meaningful conversations about literature.

- Book Scavenger Hunt: Create a scavenger hunt where students search for specific books based on clues. This can be a fun way to get students moving around the classroom and engaged in reading.

- Author Study: Choose an author and have students read several of their books. Then, have students create projects or presentations about the author's life and work.

These book exchange activities can be tailored to fit the interests and reading levels of your students. They provide opportunities for students to explore new books and authors, share their love of reading, and engage in meaningful conversations about literature.

81. Book Scavenger Hunts

Book scavenger hunts are a fun and interactive way to get students excited about reading and to help them discover new books. Here are some tips for implementing book scavenger hunts in your classroom:

- Set up clues: Create a set of clues that lead students to specific books in the classroom or library. Clues can be in the form of riddles, puzzles, or descriptions of the book's content.

- Provide instructions: Before beginning the scavenger hunt, provide students with clear instructions and expectations for how the activity will work. Be sure to explain any rules or restrictions, such as not running in the library or not removing books from the shelves.

- Organize students: Divide students into teams or pairs and assign each group a different set of clues to follow.

- Give time limits: Set a time limit for the scavenger hunt and encourage students to work quickly and efficiently to find all of the books.

- Celebrate success: Once all of the books have been found, have students gather together and share what they found. This can be a great opportunity to discuss the books and recommend them to one another.

Book scavenger hunts are a fun and engaging way to promote literacy and encourage students to explore new books. By creating a set of clues and organizing students into teams, you can help students develop problem-solving skills, teamwork, and critical thinking abilities, all while fostering a love of reading.

82. Reading Response Journals

Reading response journals are a way for students to reflect on and respond to what they have read. Here are some tips for implementing reading response journals in your classroom:

- Provide clear expectations: Explain to students what is expected in their reading response journals. For example, specify the length of the response, the types of questions to be answered, or the format of the journal.

- Offer a variety of prompts: Provide students with a range of prompts or questions to guide their responses. This can help them to think more deeply about what they have read and to generate thoughtful and meaningful responses.

- Encourage reflection: Encourage students to reflect on their reading experiences and to connect what they have read to their own lives, interests, or experiences. This can help to foster a more personal and engaging reading experience.

- Allow for student choice: Provide opportunities for students to choose their own reading materials and to respond to them in their reading response journals. This can help to increase motivation and engagement with the reading material.

- Provide feedback: Review and provide feedback on students' reading response journals. This can help to reinforce good habits and improve their reading and writing skills.

Reading response journals can be an effective way to encourage students to think more deeply about what they have read and to engage with the material in a more personal and meaningful way. By providing clear expectations, offering a variety of prompts, encouraging reflection, allowing for student choice, and providing feedback, you can help to create a positive and productive reading experience for your students.

83. Writing Response Journals

Writing response journals are a great way to encourage students to reflect on their learning and express their thoughts and ideas in written form. Here are some tips for implementing writing response journals in your classroom:

- Choose a topic or prompt: Select a topic or prompt that relates to the content you are covering in class or that encourages reflection and critical thinking.

- Provide guidelines: Provide guidelines for how long each entry should be, what format it should take (such as bullet points, paragraphs, or free-writing), and how often students should write in their journals.

- Encourage reflection: Encourage students to reflect on their learning and personal experiences related to the topic or prompt. Ask them to consider how the content applies to their lives and how it might affect their future choices and decisions.

- Give feedback: Provide feedback on students' entries, acknowledging their thoughts and ideas and providing suggestions for improvement. This can be done in writing or through in-person conferences.

- Incorporate peer review: Encourage students to read and comment on each other's journal entries, providing feedback and suggestions for improvement.

Writing response journals can be a valuable tool for promoting reflective thinking and improving writing skills. By providing guidelines, encouraging reflection, giving feedback, and incorporating peer review, you can help students to develop a deeper understanding of the content they are learning and to express their ideas and opinions in a meaningful way.

84. Interactive Blogs

- Interactive blogs are online platforms that allow readers to interact with the content by commenting, sharing, and creating content. In the context of education, interactive blogs can be used to promote communication, collaboration, and critical thinking among students.

- Teachers can create a class blog where students can share their thoughts, reflections, and opinions about the topics they are studying. They can also post multimedia content such as videos, images, and podcasts to enrich the learning experience. By allowing students to comment on each other's posts, teachers can encourage dialogue, constructive criticism, and feedback.

- Interactive blogs can also be used to promote digital literacy and media literacy. By providing students with an opportunity to create their own blog posts, teachers can teach them how to write for a digital audience, how to use multimedia to support their message, and how to evaluate the credibility of online sources.

- To implement an interactive blog activity, teachers can start by creating a blog and inviting students to join. They can provide guidelines on how to create and share content, as well as rules for commenting and providing feedback. Teachers can also use rubrics to assess the quality of the students' blog posts and comments.

- Interactive blogs can be a valuable tool for promoting active learning, communication, collaboration, and digital literacy in the classroom.

85. Interactive Wikis

- Interactive wikis are online collaborative platforms that allow users to create and edit web pages collaboratively. In the context of education, interactive wikis can be used as a platform for collaborative writing, knowledge-sharing, and knowledge co-creation among students. Students can use wikis to work together on group projects, create a shared knowledge base, or contribute to class discussions.

- To use an interactive wiki in the classroom, the teacher can set up a wiki site for the class and provide students with the login information. The teacher can then assign topics or projects for students to work on collaboratively, and the students can use the wiki to create and edit web pages related to the assigned topics.

- To ensure that the wiki is used effectively and to promote a positive collaborative environment, the teacher should establish clear guidelines and expectations for student participation. The teacher should also monitor the wiki regularly to ensure that the content is appropriate and accurate.

- An activity that can be done using an interactive wiki is to have students collaborate to create a knowledge base on a specific topic. The teacher can divide the class into groups and assign each group a different subtopic related to the main topic. The groups can then work together to create and edit web pages on the wiki related to their assigned subtopic. Once all the groups have completed their pages, the class can review the wiki as a whole to gain a comprehensive understanding of the main topic.

86. Interactive Podcasts

Interactive podcast activity for students:

- Choose a topic: Have students choose a topic they are interested in or have been studying in class. It could be a historical event, a scientific concept, a literary work, or anything else related to your curriculum.

- Research: Students should research their chosen topic thoroughly, gathering information from a variety of sources such as books, articles, and websites.

- Script writing: Have students create a script for a podcast episode, incorporating their research and any other interesting facts or anecdotes they may have come across.

- Recording: Students can then record their podcast using a microphone and a recording software such as Audacity or GarageBand. Encourage them to use sound effects and music to make their podcast more engaging.

- Editing: Once the recording is complete, students should edit their podcast, cutting out any mistakes or irrelevant information, and making sure it flows smoothly.

- Sharing: Finally, students can share their podcasts with the class or post them on a class blog or website. Encourage classmates to listen to each other's podcasts and provide feedback or ask questions.

This activity can help students develop their research, writing, and presentation skills, while also allowing them to explore their creativity and use technology in the classroom.

87. Interactive Videos

Interactive videos are an engaging way to promote active learning and student participation in the classroom. Here are some ideas for activities that can be done with interactive videos:

- Pause and Reflect: Pause the video at certain points and ask students to reflect on what they just learned. They can share their thoughts with a partner or in small groups.

- Predict and Confirm: Ask students to make a prediction about what will happen next in the video. Then, have them watch to confirm if their prediction was correct or not.

- Discussion Questions: Before watching the video, provide students with a list of discussion questions related to the topic. After watching, have students discuss their answers to the questions in small groups or as a class.

- Choose Your Own Adventure: Create an interactive video with branching paths, where students make choices that determine the direction of the video. This can be a fun way to engage students and encourage critical thinking.

- Interactive Quizzes: Include interactive quizzes within the video to check for understanding and promote active learning. These can be simple multiple-choice questions or more complex scenarios that require problem-solving skills.

- Caption It: Have students watch a video without sound and create captions that match the visuals. This can be a fun way to develop language skills and encourage creativity.

- Video Response: After watching a video, have students create a short response video where they share their thoughts, questions, and opinions on the topic. This can be a fun way to encourage public speaking skills and promote student voice.

88. Interactive Webinars

Interactive webinars are a great way to engage students in online learning. Here are some steps to create an interactive webinar activity:

- Choose a topic: Select a topic that you want to cover in the webinar. Make sure it is relevant to the students and their course content.

- Create a presentation: Create a PowerPoint presentation or any other presentation tool that you prefer. Make sure it is engaging and visually appealing.

- Add interactive elements: Add interactive elements to the presentation such as quizzes, polls, and surveys. You can use online tools like Kahoot or Mentimeter to create interactive elements.

- Practice: Practice your presentation several times to make sure that everything works smoothly.

- Schedule the webinar: Choose a date and time for the webinar and send invitations to the students.

- Conduct the webinar: Conduct the webinar on the scheduled date and time. Make sure you have a stable internet connection and test your equipment before the webinar.

- Follow-up: After the webinar, follow up with the students to get their feedback and address any questions they may have.

89. Interactive Workshops

One possible interactive workshop activity could be a design thinking workshop. In this workshop, students could be tasked with identifying and solving a real-world problem, such as reducing waste or improving access to healthy food in their community.

The workshop could be structured as follows:

- Introduction: The teacher could introduce the concept of design thinking and explain the problem that the students will be working to solve.

- Empathy: Students could conduct interviews with community members and research the problem to gain a deeper understanding of the issue.

- Define: Based on their research, students could define the problem they will be working to solve and identify key stakeholders.

- Ideate: Students could generate ideas for potential solutions to the problem, using brainstorming and other ideation techniques.

- Prototype: Students could select the most promising idea and create a prototype of their solution, using materials such as paper, cardboard, and craft supplies.

- Test: Students could test their prototype with potential users and stakeholders, gather feedback, and refine their solution.

- Presentation: Finally, students could present their solution to the class, explaining their thought process and the steps they took to arrive at their final design.

Throughout the workshop, the teacher could provide guidance and support, as well as facilitate group discussions and critiques of each other's work. This interactive and hands-on workshop would allow students to develop important skills such as problem-solving, creativity, and collaboration, while also addressing a real-world issue.

90. Interactive Seminars

One possible activity for an interactive seminar is a roundtable discussion. Here are the steps:

- Divide students into small groups of 3-5 people.

- Assign a discussion topic related to the seminar content to each group.

- Give the groups 10-15 minutes to discuss the topic and come up with a list of key points or insights.

- Bring the groups back together and have them form a larger circle.

- Each group takes turns sharing their key points or insights with the larger group.

- Encourage questions and discussion among the larger group after each group has presented.

- Wrap up the activity by summarizing the key ideas that emerged from the discussion and how they relate to the seminar content.

This activity can help students engage with the seminar content in a meaningful way, while also giving them an opportunity to share their perspectives and learn from their peers.

91. Interactive Tutorials

- Interactive tutorials are educational tools that allow students to engage with material and learn in a self-paced, interactive way. These tutorials can take many forms, including videos, interactive diagrams, and simulations, and can be used in a variety of subjects.

- An activity using interactive tutorials could involve assigning students a series of interactive tutorials to complete on a particular topic or concept. The tutorials could be assigned as homework or completed in class, and students could work individually or in small groups. After completing the tutorials, students could be asked to write a reflection on what they learned, or participate in a class discussion to share their insights and questions. This activity could be used in subjects such as science, math, or history, where interactive tutorials can help students visualize complex concepts and engage with the material in a more hands-on way.

92. Interactive Case Studies

- Interactive case studies are a learning activity that allows students to apply their knowledge and critical thinking skills to real-world scenarios. In an interactive case study, students are presented with a complex problem or situation that requires analysis and decision-making. They are then asked to work in groups or individually to identify possible solutions and recommend a course of action based on the information provided.

- To make the case study interactive, teachers can provide students with additional resources, such as videos, articles, or expert interviews, to help them understand the context and complexity of the problem. Students can also be asked to present their solutions to the class or participate in a debate or discussion to explore different perspectives and alternatives.

- Interactive case studies can be used in various subjects, from business and economics to medicine and law, to help students develop critical thinking skills and practical problem-solving abilities. They can also be adapted to different learning styles and levels, from middle school to graduate programs.

93. Interactive Surveys

An interactive survey activity:

- Choose a topic related to the subject matter of the lesson.

- Create a survey using a tool such as Google Forms or SurveyMonkey. The survey should include questions that require critical thinking and analysis.

- In class, divide students into small groups.

- Provide each group with a link to the survey.

- Instruct each group to work together to analyze the survey questions and provide thoughtful, well-reasoned answers.

- After a set period of time, bring the groups back together and facilitate a discussion about the survey results.

- Ask each group to share their answers and compare their findings with the class.

- Lead a class discussion to explore the results and the implications of the findings.

For example, in a history class, a teacher might create a survey asking students to analyze the causes of a particular historical event, such as the American Civil War. Students would work together to provide well-reasoned answers to the survey questions and then share their findings with the class. The teacher could then facilitate a discussion about the results of the survey and how they might inform our understanding of the historical event.

94. Interactive Quizzes

- Interactive quizzes are a great way to engage students and assess their knowledge in an interactive way. They can be used in a variety of subject areas and are particularly useful for testing students' understanding of key concepts or vocabulary.

- One way to create an interactive quiz is to use an online quiz platform, such as Kahoot, Quizlet, or Google Forms. These platforms allow you to create quizzes with multiple-choice, true/false, or short answer questions, and can provide immediate feedback to students. Some platforms even allow students to compete with one another in real-time, which can add an extra level of engagement.

- Another way to create interactive quizzes is to use game-based learning platforms, such as Classcraft or ClasscraftEDU. These platforms allow you to create quizzes with game-like elements, such as points, badges, and leaderboards. This can make the quiz more engaging and motivate students to participate.

To create an effective interactive quiz, it is important to consider the following tips:

- Keep it short and focused: Limit the number of questions and make sure they are all related to the same topic or concept.

- Make it visually appealing: Use images, videos, or other media to make the quiz more engaging.

- Provide immediate feedback: Let students know whether they got the answer right or wrong, and provide an explanation for the correct answer.

- Make it interactive: Use game-like elements or real-time feedback to make the quiz more engaging.

- Use it as a formative assessment: Use the results of the quiz to inform your instruction and provide targeted feedback to students.

Interactive quizzes can be a great tool for engaging students and assessing their knowledge in a fun and engaging way.

95. Interactive Games

Interactive games refer to activities that involve playing games to help students learn and practice new concepts. These games can be played in person or online and can cover a wide range of subjects, including math, science, history, and more. Interactive games can be a fun and engaging way for students to learn and reinforce concepts, while also promoting critical thinking and problem-solving skills.

Some examples of interactive games include:

- Jeopardy-style games

- Kahoot quizzes

- Trivia games

- Escape room activities

- Digital board games

- Crossword puzzles

- Sudoku puzzles

- Word search puzzles

- Role-playing games

These games can be customized to fit the specific needs and interests of the students, and can be used to supplement classroom lectures and activities.

96. Interactive Challenges

- Interactive challenges are activities that challenge learners to apply their knowledge or skills in a fun and engaging way. These activities can take many forms, such as quizzes, puzzles, games, simulations, and more.

- For example, an interactive challenge could be a crossword puzzle that reinforces vocabulary words from a recent lesson. Another example could be a simulation that allows students to practice decision-making skills in a real-world context.

- The goal of interactive challenges is to provide learners with an opportunity to actively engage with the content and practice their skills in a way that is enjoyable and motivating. By incorporating interactive challenges into the learning process, educators can enhance student engagement and promote deeper learning.

97. Interactive Assessments

Interactive assessments refer to any method of evaluating learning outcomes that requires active participation and engagement from learners. These assessments can be used to measure a variety of skills, such as critical thinking, problem-solving, and creativity. Some examples of interactive assessments include:

- Collaborative projects: This can include group research projects or group presentations where learners work together to complete a task.

- Interactive quizzes and tests: These assessments often include interactive elements like drag-and-drop questions, matching exercises, and fill-in-the-blank questions.

- Simulations: Interactive simulations allow learners to engage in a realistic scenario and make decisions based on their learning.

- Role-playing: This can include simulations that require learners to assume a particular role, such as a manager, employee, or customer.

- Case studies: Interactive case studies require learners to analyze and solve problems based on real-life scenarios.

- Peer assessment: Peer assessment allows learners to evaluate their peers' work and provide feedback, which can help improve critical thinking and communication skills.

- Self-assessment: Self-assessment activities can help learners reflect on their learning and identify areas where they need improvement.

Interactive assessments can be an effective way to engage learners and promote active learning, allowing them to demonstrate their understanding in a more practical and engaging way.

98. Interactive Experiments

Interactive experiments are activities that engage learners in the scientific process of inquiry and experimentation. They involve hands-on experiences that allow students to manipulate variables, collect data, and analyze results. These types of activities help students develop their critical thinking, problem-solving, and scientific reasoning skills. Interactive experiments can take many forms, from simple activities that can be done in a classroom or lab to more complex projects that involve specialized equipment or resources. Some examples of interactive experiments include:

- Building and testing bridges to determine their strength and stability.

- Investigating the effects of different fertilizers on plant growth.

- Conducting experiments on the properties of light and sound.

- Studying the effects of temperature, pressure, and other factors on chemical reactions.

- Observing the behavior of insects or other animals in a controlled environment.

To make these experiments more interactive, educators can provide opportunities for students to collaborate, share ideas, and reflect on their experiences. For example, students could work in teams to design and carry out their own experiments, then present their findings to the class.

They could also use digital tools and resources to enhance their learning and share their work with a wider audience.

99. Interactive Research Studies

An interactive research study activity:

- Introduction: Begin by introducing the research study and explaining its purpose.

- Group Formation: Divide students into groups of four or five and assign each group a research topic.

- Research: Give the groups time to research their topics and collect data. Encourage them to use a variety of sources, such as books, websites, and interviews.

- Design Experiment: Have each group design an experiment to test a hypothesis related to their research topic.

- Conduct Experiment: Allow the groups time to conduct their experiments and collect data.

- Analyze Data: Have the groups analyze their data and draw conclusions about their hypotheses.

- Share Results: Ask each group to present their findings to the class, including the research question, hypothesis, experiment design, data collected, and conclusions.

- Discuss: Engage the class in a discussion about the research studies and the conclusions drawn. Encourage students to ask questions, share their thoughts and opinions, and consider the implications of the research for the real world.

- Reflection: End the activity with a reflection exercise where students can write about what they learned from the research studies and the interactive activity.

By conducting interactive research studies activity, students are able to apply critical thinking skills to a real-world situation, collaborate in groups to gather and analyze data, and communicate their findings effectively to the class.

100. Interactive Surveys

An interactive survey:

- Choose a topic for your survey, such as favorite food, favorite movie genre, or preferred vacation destination.

- Create a survey using an online tool like Google Forms or SurveyMonkey.

- Share the survey with your class or group and ask them to complete it.

- Once everyone has completed the survey, analyze the data and create a graph or chart to show the results.

- Discuss the results as a group, asking questions like: "Were there any surprises in the results?" "Did anyone's responses stand out?" "What patterns do you see in the data?"

This activity can help students develop skills in data analysis and interpretation, as well as critical thinking and discussion. It also allows for creativity in choosing survey topics and designing the survey questions.

101. Interactive Feedback Loops

An interactive feedback loop activity:

- Ask students to work on a writing task, such as drafting an essay or a short story.

- After they finish writing, ask them to pair up and read each other's work.

- Instruct them to give feedback to their partner using a feedback form that includes a list of questions about specific elements of writing, such as organization, grammar, and structure.

- Ask students to discuss their feedback with each other and revise their writing based on the feedback they received.

- Once they have revised their writing, ask them to share their revised work with the class.

- Provide an opportunity for the class to give feedback on the revised writing and discuss what they learned from the process.

- Finally, ask students to reflect on the feedback they received and how it helped them improve their writing.

This activity allows students to receive feedback from multiple sources and make revisions based on that feedback. It also provides an opportunity for students to engage in peer review and learn from each other.